# BREAKING NEWS
# ALL OVER AGAIN

## *The History Behind Today's Headlines*

BY

## Ronald G. Shafer

Author, *The Carnival Campaign:*
*How The Rollicking 1840 Campaign of "Tippecanoe and*
*Tyler Too" Changed Presidential Elections Forever*

Published 2022 in Williamsburg, Va., by Ronald G. Shafer
Retropolis columns with permission the Washington Post
Photos from the Library of Congress

Published 2022

*To my inspiring wife, Mary*

*"Those that fail to learn from history are doomed to repeat it."*
*– Winston Churchill*

*"There's an old saying about those who forget history. I don't remember it, but it's good."*
*– Stephen Colbert*

# TABLE OF CONTENTS

Introduction................................................................. ix

Chapter One
          Abigail Adams's "Fearsome" Decision ...........................1
Chapter Two
          There Was Nothing Spanish About The "Spanish Flu."...7
Chapter Three
          The Fakc Flu Nurse ........................................................11
Chapter Four
          Campaigning From Home .................................................15
Chapter Five
          The First Televised Conventions ...................................21
Chapter Six:
          The First Presidential Campaign With Women .............27
Chapter Seven
          The Ugliest Presidential Election In History.................33
Chapter Eight
          The "Mississippi Plan" And Voter Suppression ...........39
Chapter Nine
          Why A Veep Can't Decide A Presidential Election ........43
Chapter Ten
          The Vice President's Enslaved Wife..............................49
Chapter Eleven
          The First Presidential Impeachment Try And Tyler Too....55
Chapter Twelve
          Barricaded In His Office................................................59
Chapter Thirteen
          Guess Who's Not Coming To The Inauguration ...........65

Chapter Fourteen
     A Turbulent Transition.................................................71
Chapter Fifteen
     Grover Cleveland Returns ..............................................75
Chapter Sixteen
     The First Investigation Of A Capitol Attack...................79
Chapter Seventeen
     Tempest In A Teapot Dome ............................................85
Chapter Eighteen
     With Malice Toward None...............................................91
Chapter Nineteen
     America's First Columbus Day .......................................97
Chapter Twenty
     Happy Franksgiving .....................................................103
Chapter Twenty-One
     Santa Wore Blue ..........................................................107

About The Author .........................................................113
Other books by Ron Shafer...............................................115

# INTRODUCTION

Over a journalism career that began on the Ohio State University student newspaper, the Lantern, through 38 years at the Wall Street Journal, I was able to observe many historical events. They ranged from the colorful to the tragic.

In 1961 I marched with students in Columbus, Ohio, to report on their protest of the OSU faculty rejecting an invitation for the undefeated football team to play in the Rose Bowl. In my first year at the Journal in Chicago in 1963, I interviewed shocked people on the street moments after the assassination of President John F. Kennedy.

In 1964 in Detroit, I wrote about the introduction of Ford's new sporty car, the Mustang. In 1967, I drove my red Mustang convertible through the deserted streets of Detroit following a riot, and in 1968 I witnessed more riots in Washington, D.C. after the murder of the Rev. Martin Luther King Jr.

I saw protests in Washington against President Lyndon B. Johnson's Vietnam War policies. I was there during Watergate when President Richard M. Nixon resigned. I wrote about local golfer Lee Elder's successful drive to become the first Black golfer in the Master's golf tournament.

I was an eyewitness at presidential conventions that nominated Jimmy Carter, Walter Mondale, Ronald Reagan, Bill Clinton and Al Gore. With the reporting of the Journal's talented staff, for more than 15 years I wrote about inside news from the capital in the page-one Washington Wire column.

After retiring to Williamsburg, Va., I wrote about history in a book on the 1840 presidential campaign of two local men, William Henry Harrison and John Tyler – better known as "Tippecanoe and Tyler Too." I wrote a book about the start of the Brooklyn Dodgers and their first pennant-winning manager Bill "Gunner" McGunnigle – the great-grandfather of my wife, Mary Rogers.

Then as a free-lance writer I discovered the Retropolis column in the Washington Post. Retropolis, "the past, rediscovered," ties current events with past ones. This collection of my Retropolis stories focuses on two major events – the deadly coronavirus pandemic, and the presidential election of 2020 and its aftermath. My article about a vice president who had an enslaved wife was the most read Retropolis column in 2021.

With thanks to my Retropolis editors Lynda Robinson and Aaron Wiener,

Ron Shafer, Williamsburg, Va.

# CHAPTER ONE

# ABIGAIL ADAMS'S "FEARSOME" DECISION

By Ronald G. Shafer
*This column was published in the Washington Post on Dec. 14, 2020*

The future first lady feared inoculation, but she feared smallpox more.

It was 1776, and Abigail Adams had decided that she and her four children would seek protection from a deadly epidemic. Her husband, John Adams, was in Philadelphia, where the Declaration of Independence had just been announced.

A smallpox inoculation involved a controversial treatment: infecting the recipient with a mild case of the deadly disease. "God grant that we may all go comfortably through the Distemper," Abigail wrote her husband.

At the dawn of the American Revolution, the world was fighting smallpox just as it now is battling the novel coronavirus. Like the novel coronavirus, smallpox was "a highly contagious virus that is transmitted from contact with an infected person, causing illness," said Jonathan Stolz, a retired physician in Williamsburg, Va., and author of "Medicine from Cave Dwellers to Millennials." More than 100,000 people in the colonies died of smallpox. Scientists around the world were desperately seeking to develop a vaccine.

People are now beginning to receive vaccines to prevent covid-19, the illness caused by the coronavirus. In 1776, the only medical preventive was an inoculation that had been developed in Boston in the 1720s by Cotton Mather, a Puritan minister, and Zabdiel Boylston, a physician, and was based on techniques shown to them by enslaved Africans, including one of Mather's enslaved men, Onesimus.

But the procedure was considered so dangerous that a number of states eventually banned it. So many people ignored the ban, however, that in June 1776, Massachusetts suspended its prohibition, and many doctors set up shop in Boston to perform inoculations.

Abigail Adams headed to Boston with her four children — 11-year-old Abigail (called "Nabby"), John Quincy, age 9; Charles, age 6, and 4-year-old Thomas. She had the support of her husband, who had gone through the painful process of inoculation in 1764 and wanted his family protected.

It was "a fearsome decision," wrote presidential historian Feather Schwartz Foster in her book, "The First Ladies." The treatment involved scraping a smallpox-infected serum into the skin. If the procedure were successful, pock marks would occur in about 10 days. The term "small pocks" led to the name smallpox.

Abigail and her children "went ten miles from their home in Braintree to Boston, to be inoculated by Dr. Thomas Bullfinch, an expert at the procedure," Foster wrote.

Several thousand people had flocked to Boston. "Such a spirit of inoculation never before took place, the Town and every House in it, are as full as they can hold," Mrs. Adams wrote her husband.

"I had many disagreeable Sensations at the Thoughts of coming myself, but to see my children through it I thought my duty, and all those feelings vanished as soon as I was inoculated, and I trust a kind providence will carry me safely through."

FIGURE 1 ABIGAIL ADAMS

The family was inoculated on July 12. "Our Little ones stood the operation Manfully," Mrs. Adams wrote. "The Little folks are very sick then and puke every morning, but after that they are comfortable."

Then came the wait to see whether the procedure had worked. Abigail, addressing her husband as "my dearest Friend," wrote that Nabby and Johnny were showing signs of the disease as planned but that Tommy wasn't, so the doctor "inoculated him again today fearing it had not taken."

By July 29, Mrs. Adams was able to report about herself, "I write you now, thanks be to Heaven, free from pain, in Good Spirits, but weak and feeble." But she noted that "the smallpox acts very oddly this Season ... 3 out of our 4 children have been twice inoculated, two of them Charles and Tommy have not had one Symptom."

Future president John Quincy was having the easiest case, said historian Foster. But "Nabby Adams was very sick with fevers, terrible body aches, and erupting pustules," Foster wrote. "Neither Charles and Thomas responded to the inoculation, and it had to be repeated.

For Charles, it had to be repeated three times — the last, with a more 'active' scraping, ensuring that he would contract the dreaded disease as if he had contracted it naturally."

Abigail had hoped to complete the entire treatment in three weeks. But the doctors were experiencing a high failure rate, requiring extra time for results. "Every physician has a number of patients in this doubtful state," she wrote her husband.

John Adams agonized between letters. "I hang upon Tenterhooks" for reports, he wrote. And he was angered to hear about the delays in treatment.

In an Aug. 3 letter, he complained that the doctors had taken on too many patients. "No Physician has either Head or Hands enough to attend a Thousand Patients...I wish you had all come to Philadelphia and had the Distemper here."

Mrs. Adams wrote that Nabby was so sore "that she can neither walk sit stand or lie with any comfort." But "at present all my attention is taken up with the care of our Little Charles who has been very bad. The Symptoms rose to a burning fever... and delirium ensued for 48 hours."

Finally, on Aug. 31, Mrs. Adams reported that a friend had taken all of the children except "our Little Charles who is weak and feeble."

By Sept. 2, Charles, too, was on the way to recovery." This is a Beautiful Morning," Abigail wrote her husband. "I came here with all my treasure of children, have passed through one of the most terrible Diseases to which human Nature is subject, and not one of us is wanting."

The smallpox epidemic continued to devastate the economy of the colonies and preparations for war against the British. Gen. George Washington, who had recovered from smallpox and thus was immune, was an early advocate of inoculation.

In 1777, "Washington had all his troops and incoming recruits inoculated," Stolz said. "The government-sponsored mass inoculation was the first of its kind in America."

Finally, in 1798, the British physician Edward Jenner announced a vaccine, originally using cowpox, that would prevent smallpox.

Jenner declared that "the annihilation of the smallpox, the most dreadful scourge of the human species, must be the final result of this practice." Eventually, smallpox was eradicated around the world.

In 1802, the American Academy of Arts and Sciences in Boston unanimously voted to make Jenner a member. A letter of congratulations was sent to Jenner from the academy's corresponding secretary, smallpox-inoculation survivor John Quincy Adams. In 1825, Adams became the sixth president of the United States.

By then, his mother, Abigail, had died of a different scourge that wouldn't have a vaccine until the end of the 19th century: typhoid fever.

# CHAPTER TWO

# THERE WAS NOTHING SPANISH ABOUT THE "SPANISH FLU."

By Ronald G. Shafer
*This column was published in the Washington
Post on March 23, 2020*

Don't call it the Spanish flu.

That's what Spain said in 1918 at the start of what would become the deadliest pandemic in history, killing more than 50 million people worldwide. The Spanish got tagged with the killer name during the end of World War I because Spain was the first country to report the disease publicly, not because it originated there.

Spaniards called the highly contagious disease "The Soldier of Naples" after a catchy song popular at the time. But when the deadly virus exploded across the world and became known as "Spanish influenza," Spain protested that its people were being falsely stigmatized.

President Trump is sparking similar complaints by referring to the coronavirus as the "Chinese virus" because it probably started in Wuhan, China. Critics say the president is unfairly stigmatizing all Chinese people, while the president contends he is just stating facts.

In 2015, the World Health Organization issued new guidelines for naming diseases "to minimize unnecessary negative impact of disease names" and "avoid causing offense to any cultural, social, national, regional, professional or ethnic groups." The WHO specifically counseled against referring to countries in disease names.

That guidance came much too late to help Spain.

As World War I was winding down, a deadly pandemic had erupted in several countries, but under wartime censorship, the news was kept secret. Spain was neutral in the war, and Spanish officials made the mistake of cabling London to say that "a strange form of disease of epidemic character has appeared in Madrid."

London newspapers jumped on the story, calling the illness the Spanish influenza or the Spanish grip, because the symptoms resembled the French grippe.

At first, the news was not taken seriously. "When flu bowled over the good señors and señoritas of Madrid, there was a panic," wrote one London journalist. Before long, "flu had its run in Spain and was soon found to be a gentle, jolly little disease — almost sporty."

As flu casualties skyrocketed in Europe and the United States, a Spanish medical official protested the Spanish name connection in an Oct 1, 1919, "Letter from Madrid" published in the Bulletin of the American Medical Association. The disease in Spain was "sudden in its appearance, brief in its course and subsiding without leaving a trace," the official wrote.

When the epidemic began ravaging other countries, he wrote, "we were surprised to learn" people were calling it "the Spanish grip. ... The germ may have increased its virulences and its power of diffusion in Spain, but it is evident that this epidemic was not born in Spain."

By then, nations were pointing fingers at one another. Spain also called the virus the "French flu," claiming French visitors to Madrid had brought it. "Germans called it the Russian Pest," wrote Kenneth C. Davis in his book, "More Deadly Than War." In a precursor to today's crisis, "The Russians called it the Chinese Flu."

Many people "leaped to the conclusion that this new evil, like early evils, must be traced to Germany," one newspaper reported. The New York Times quoted a U.S. Army official who speculated that germs might have been planted by enemy agents put ashore from German submarines off the East Coast: "It would be quite easy for one of these German agents to turn loose Spanish influenza germs in a theater or some other place where large numbers of persons are assembled." There were even rumors that the germ was being put in Bayer aspirin.

Spain's protest was overwhelmed by the media reports and the public culture. The disease also became known as "The Spanish Lady." A poster showed a skeleton-like woman, clad in a veil and a long, dark dress, holding a handkerchief and a Flamenco fan. One implication: She was a prostitute, spreading her infection worldwide.

Medical advertising also ran with the Spanish theme. One ad declared that medical authorities said the disease "is simply the old fashioned grip. ... This time it comes by way of Spain." The best way to stay safe? "Above all, avoid colds. Use Vicks VaporRub at the very first sign of a cold."

The clincher was the announcement in early October that Spain's King Alfonso XIII had come down with the flu, along with several members of his cabinet. Spanish officials repudiated any claims that the illness was a "Spanish disease," adding that if Americans didn't take care, "the epidemic will become so widespread throughout the United States that soon we shall hear the disease called 'American' influenza."

Many prominent people in the United States and other countries caught the disease. In September 1918, Secretary of the Navy Franklin D. Roosevelt was taken by ambulance from the USS Leviathan, which had just docked in New York City, after getting the pneumonia that often followed the flu. Others who caught it included President Woodrow Wilson, British Prime Minister David Lloyd George, Mohandas Gandhi, Groucho Marx and Walt Disney.

The pandemic lasted until the end of 1920. In the United States, the flu killed more than 675,000 people. Speculation about the disease's origin continued.

In 1920, after war censorship was lifted, reports suggested that the U.S. outbreak began among Army soldiers training at Camp Funston on Fort Riley in Kansas, where 46 people had died of resulting pneumonia.

# CHAPTER THREE

# THE FAKE FLU NURSE

By Ronald G. Shafer
*This column was published in the Washington Post on May 17, 2020*

Julia Lyons portrayed herself as a busy visiting nurse in Chicago during the great flu pandemic of 1918. But "Slick Julia," as she came to be known, was no Florence Nightingale.

The 23-year-old Julia, "a woman of diamonds and furs, silken ankles, gem-studded fingers and aliases by the dozens," was posing as a "flu nurse," ripping off home-bound patients for cash and jewelry as they suffered and even died, the Chicago Tribune reported in late 1918. "With her rose-lipped smile and pearly teeth," she "performed various miracles at getting ready money."

A century before the coronavirus crisis, the 1918 flu was a killing machine, taking the lives of more than 675,000 people in the United States and 50 million around the world. Just as in the current pandemic, nurses were on the front line caring for the sick. Chicago, like other cities, was desperate for nurses to care for victims in their homes.

Julia Lyons saw an opportunity. Figuring nobody would have time to check her lack of credentials, she signed on at as home-nurse registry under various names. In late 1918, the Tribune chronicled the fake flu nurse's escapades like a dime detective novel.

"While influenza patients died or lived, Julia, clad in nurse's uniform, plundered their homes," the paper reported. After one woman called for a nurse, Julia went to the drug store for her to fill a prescription for oxygen that cost $5 but told her patient it cost $63, equal to $85 and $1,077 today. "Julia tarried briefly, taking when she flew two rings, two lady's suits, a pair of oxfords and a breast pin."

Sometimes she worked with an accomplice. "In comes an M.D. known to the police as a dope seller and narcotic supplier," the Tribune wrote. "He writes a prescription; she hustles out and gets it filled. The family is stung for $25 for what proves to be a dime's worth of Cherryola."

When one elderly man became suspicious, Julia turned on her charm.

"Don't you remember me? Why when I was a little girl I used to hitch on your wagons." The man used to have wagons. He couldn't exactly place her, the Tribune reported, "but it made it mighty easy to touch him for $28 for oxygen and $22 for the Cherryola."

When police detectives came calling, the man, "right horrified at the idea that this beautiful, smiling, pearly teethed model nurse might be a crook of the deepest dye," said: "Why I've known her for twenty years. When she was a little girl, she used to hitch on my wagons."

"That night Julia vanished, taking for further good measure a wristwatch, some money and certain other things." The next day, the man told the detective, "By golly, I guess I was wrong."

The cops finally traced Julia via a friend named Eva Jacobs, who lived in a flat with "Suicide Bess" Davis, a con woman. The house was known as a "hangout for thieves," the Tribune wrote.

The police tapped the phone and learned Julia lived nearby. Detectives trailed Julia. One day she set off to marry Charlie the Greek, who ran the Victory Restaurant on West Madison Avenue. Before vows could be exchanged, Julia was in handcuffs.

"How long you known this dame?" said one detective to Charlie at the jail.

"Ten days!" replied Charlie. "That is, I thought I knew her."

That night Julia and Eva slept in adjoining cells. "We thought it was easy money," said Eva — the phone tap revealing they were partners.

The next day in the police station Julia came face to face with the widow of a former patient the fake nurse had abandoned. "You killed my husband! There is no punishment too terrible for you," the woman cried. Julia was arraigned under charges of larceny, running a confidence game and obtaining money under false pretenses.

But "Slick Julia" wasn't done. The next day Deputy Sheriff John Hickey volunteered to take Julia from the county jail to court. One detective on the case advised Hickey: "Keep your eyes peeled. She's pretty slippery. Better put irons on her."

"Oh, she won't get away," Hickey said.

Instead of transporting Julia to the courthouse in a patrol wagon, the deputy sheriff took her on a street car. In court, some 50 victims testified against her. She was held under $13,000 bond, the equivalent of more than $190,000 today.

Deputy Hickey started back to the county jail with Julia in tow. An hour and a half later he called the police and "excitedly" told them she had jumped from a moving street car and hopped into a waiting automobile. Based on the reported location, one official speculated Hickey and his prisoner had been going to cabarets.

Hickey then changed his story to say Julia wanted to go to a bank to withdraw money. While there, he said, "I turned around for just a second — and Julia was gone." That night Hickey was jailed on suspicion of accepting a payoff.

Soon Julia was back at her old tricks. In March 1919, the police traced her through the nurse registry to a home on Fullerton Boulevard. When Julia answered the door, the police nabbed her.

"Flu Julia," who "walked away one November day from former Deputy Sheriff John Hickey, walked back into custody, involuntarily last night," the Tribune reported.

She faced a new charge — her 20th — bigamy. Though already married, Julia had gotten hitched to a young soldier.

"I met him while clerking in a delicatessen on the south side," Julia said. "It was so romantic. We only knew each other four days when I became his bride. We went to papa's farm on our honeymoon."

Finally, in April Julia went on trial for larceny. She testified "she had been the victim of a band of thieves who had forced her to commit acts against her will," the Tribune reported. She even fainted in court to show her distress.

The jury didn't buy it. Before sentencing, Julia pleaded insanity, but physicians testified she wasn't insane. In July, "Slick Julia," the fake flu nurse, was sent to the state penitentiary for one to 10 years.

# CHAPTER FOUR

# CAMPAIGNING FROM HOME

By Ronald G. Shafer
*This column was published in the Washington Post on May 3, 2020*

"If you want to be elected, stay at home during the campaign," a U.S. senator from Colorado joked to the presidential candidate.

"That fits right in my idea," replied Sen. Warren G. Harding (R-Ohio). In 1920, Harding ran the last "front porch" campaign by a U.S. presidential candidate from his home at 380 Mount Vernon Ave. in Marion, just north of Columbus.

A century later, presumptive Democratic presidential nominee Joe Biden is challenging President Trump from the basement of his Delaware home, where he has been sheltering in place during the coronavirus pandemic. Trump is preparing to head out of the White House for the first time in weeks, starting with a weekend trip to Camp David.

Both men are itching to get out on the campaign trail with rallies and speeches. Harding's goal was exactly the opposite: "to restore the dignity of the office" of president by avoiding the "barnstorming, water tank speech and [railroad-car] tail end platform business."

Presidential candidates not only sat home but didn't even campaign before 1840, when Ohio's William Henry "Old Tippecanoe" Harrison became the first to give speeches with a campaign of carnival-like rallies. In 1880, Republican James Garfield campaigned from his farm in Mentor, Ohio. In 1888, Republican Benjamin Harrison, William Henry's grandson, ran from his house in Indianapolis. Harding patterned his campaign after Republican William McKinley, who in 1896 campaigned from his front porch in Canton, Ohio.

Republicans nominated the 54-year-old Harding, the publisher of the Marion Star newspaper, at their Chicago convention on the 10th ballot. The handsome, silver-haired senator had one thing going for him, his campaign manager said. "He looked like a president." His running mate was Massachusetts Gov. Calvin Coolidge.

Harding's campaign theme was "a return to normalcy" after the turmoil of World War I and the 1918 flu pandemic.

Instead of going to the people, he had the people come to the large, curving front porch of his wood-frame house in Marion, a town of about 30,000 residents.

Visitors paraded through town to the house, where crowds often numbering in the thousands sat in chairs or stood on the front lawn. The plush green grass had been replaced by white crushed limestone. The flagpole from McKinley's home was planted in the Harding yard.

At the first gathering in mid-July, an airplane flew over the house and dropped a floral wreath. Harding gave a speech calling for unity. A headline in one Montana newspaper declared: "On Front Porch, Harding Voices His Platitudes."

The reviews soon got better. Visitors ranged from political and business leaders to Civil War veterans and 3,000 traveling salesmen. In August, members of women's groups joined Harding to celebrate ratification of women's suffrage. "I rejoice with you," Harding said.

Later, Harding made news by promising to create a Department of Public Welfare. He hinted that he would name a woman to the Cabinet post. He called for "equal pay for equal work."

Another day five delegations of "Negro Republicans," including several Baptist ministers, came to the porch. The visitors pleaded for an end to lynching.

Drawing one of the biggest crowds was the appearance of Broadway performers joined by the "Harding Porch Jazz Band." Famed singer Al Jolson emceed. Invoking the image of Theodore Roosevelt, Jolson sang, "We think the country is ready, for another man like Teddy," and, "We need another Lincoln, to do the nation's thinkin'."

The Chicago Cubs visited Harding, and baseball fans followed. In his speech, Harding pressed his case in baseball terms. He said

Democratic President Woodrow Wilson had "muffed disappointingly in our domestic affairs and then struck out in Paris" trying to create a League of Nations.

The affable Harding and his wife, Florence, eagerly shook hands. Florence Harding, known as "the Duchess," posed for an estimated 10,000 photographs.

FIGURE 2 WARREN & FLORENCE HARDING

The porch campaign peaked in mid-October, when 50,000 people paraded to a ceremony honoring first-time voters, including women, college students and immigrants. More than two dozen bands serenaded Harding for two hours. College cheerleaders sitting on the porch roof and perched in trees led the crowd in singing campaign songs.

Meantime, Harding's Democratic rival, Ohio Gov. James Cox, was campaigning by train in 36 of the 48 states. Cox was the publisher of the Dayton Daily News, and his running mate was New York's Franklin D. Roosevelt.

Cox said he was "carrying his front porch" to the country, while his opponent continued "his self-isolation in a small Ohio community," the New York Times reported. Cox claimed Harding was "wiggling and waggling" on the top issue of the day: whether the United States should join the League of Nations.

Harding left his front porch on occasion, speaking in 16 towns in Iowa and Nebraska. In Des Moines, he declared his view on the League of Nations: "I favor staying out." His policy, he said, was "America first."

By October, Harding was far in the lead. His front-porch campaign had drawn more than 600,000 people. He eventually went on a two-week speaking tour to the South and New York and through Ohio to help Republican House and Senate candidates.

There was one more speech in Marion on Nov. 5, when thousands of supporters stormed the Harding porch to celebrate the senator's landslide victory.

Harding didn't make it to the end of his first term. In the summer of 1923, after a bout of flu, the president took a cross-country train trip. On Aug. 2 in San Francisco, he died after a heart attack.

Harding's legacy was tarnished by scandal following his death. In 1922, it was revealed that his interior secretary secretly sold drilling rights to federal oil wells in Teapot Dome, Wyo., to private oil interests.

In 1927, young Nan Britton published a book claiming she was Harding's mistress and gave birth to his daughter. Decades later, love letters were uncovered showing, in a Stormy Daniels-like moment, the Republican Party in 1920 had paid another Harding high-society mistress to take a long voyage until the election was over.

None of this was known to the public when more than 100,000 people, led by President Coolidge, flocked to Marion for Harding's funeral. At the house with the famous front porch, the Associated Press reported, "Only a flag which fluttered idly at half mast gave indication that the man who left the home he loved to accept the greatest honor a country may give him was dead."

FIGURE 3 THE HARDING PORCH MARION, OHIO

# CHAPTER FIVE

# THE FIRST TELEVISED CONVENTIONS

By Ronald G. Shafer
*This column was published in the Washington Post on Aug. 16, 2020*

At the first widely televised political convention in 1948, a smiling Clare Boothe Luce stepped to the microphone with her blonde curls and white pearls shining under the bright lights. To delegates inside Philadelphia's Municipal Auditorium, the former Republican congresswoman looked perfect.

But on black-and-white television screens, "her face, hair and dress were all one washed-out color and her gestures seeming ill-matched and awkward," one columnist wrote.

FIGURE 4 CLARE BOOTHE LUCE

The TV cameras transformed Republican presidential nominee Thomas Dewey's five o'clock shadow into "a full beard, something like Abraham Lincoln's," another columnist wrote. If speakers "could see themselves as the television audience does, they'd sit down and weep."

In the hot, non-air-conditioned hall in July, "the intense light demanded by those primitive television cameras raised dark patches of sweat" on the speakers and their clothing, NBC News President Reuven Frank wrote years later.

FIGURE 5 1948 PHILADELPHIA CONVENTIONS

This week, TV networks will be facing new kinds of challenges adjusting convention coverage because of the coronavirus pandemic. The Democrats, who'd planned to gather in Milwaukee from Monday through Thursday, plan a nearly virtual convention to nominate former vice president Joe Biden. He and his running mate, Sen. Kamala D. Harris of California, will deliver their speeches at the Chase Center in Wilmington, Del.

The Republicans moved their convention from Charlotte, to Jacksonville, Fla., but sharply curtailed events there. President Trump will probably deliver his acceptance speech from the White House on Aug. 27.

The 2020 Democratic and Republican presidential nominating conventions will be held online. It may be the biggest adjustment for the broadcasters since the transfer from radio to TV coverage 72 years ago.

Back then the "radio boys" looked down on the "TV kids." CBS had a hard time persuading its radio news star Edward R. Murrow to also do some TV commentary.

"Visuals" suddenly were in demand. During her speech, Luce waved a steak and a carton of milk to protest rising prices. CBS's Don Hewitt, later the executive producer of "60 Minutes," "raced into the hall — down two narrow flights and through the security guards — to retrieve" Luce's props "and give them to Ed Murrow, who waved them at the home audience a second time," NBC's Frank said.

Experimental TV coverage had begun at the 1940 and 1944 conventions. But 1948 saw the first regional coverage with the major TV networks beaming pictures to 18 stations along the East Coast.

FIGURE 6 EDWARD R. MURROW, ERIC SEVEREID

Life magazine sponsored NBC's gavel-to-gavel coverage, even taking over the news department. NBC's parent company, the Radio Corporation of America, was more interested in selling its new RCA Victor television sets, advertised as providing "an eye witness" to the political conventions. A 10-inch model went for $325, equal to about $3,500 today. There were about 35,000 TV sets in the United States.

The TV coverage gave Americans their first look inside the political conventions, including the colorful demonstrations when a candidate is nominated. This, too, backfired. Many Americans, wrote New York Times columnist Arthur Krock, were shocked to see that nominees for president of the United States "are chosen in a mixed setting of country circus, street carnival, medicine show and Fourth of July picnic.

The Democrats took note of the challenges for their convention two weeks later, also in Philadelphia in order to use the same TV equipment. In contrast to Luce, California Rep. Helen Gahagan Douglas, a former movie actress, showed up in her best Hollywood makeup for her convention speech.

The Democrats stationed six makeup people below the speakers' stand to apply TV touch-ups. Some veteran male politicians still balked. The convention chairman, House Speaker Sam Rayburn of Texas, spurned advice to apply makeup to his shiny bald head. But he went bareheaded in the sun for several weeks before the convention to develop a camera-friendly tan.

The televised convention culminated in a seven-hour marathon session the night that President Harry Truman was both nominated and gave an acceptance speech. At 5:45 p.m. TV cameras showed NBC's David Brinkley describing Truman's departure from Union Station in Washington. In Philadelphia, the president cooled his heels for more than four hours as friends and foes vied for TV face time inside the convention hall.

First, pro-segregation delegates from Mississippi and Alabama stormed off the floor in protest of Truman's civil rights plan. As one Alabama newspaper explained, "the nation's camera lens and television screens had to be served." Later when Truman was officially nominated, delegates celebrated on the convention floor before the cameras for 38 minutes.

By the time the president entered the hall to give his acceptance speech, it was 1:43 a.m., not exactly prime time. Before Rayburn could introduce Truman, there was one more bit of TV business. A woman opened several cartons and out flew 48 white doves, one for each state.

The doves flew up toward the fans in the rafters. Many of the birds kept flying back to the speaker's stand, where an angry Rayburn kept picking them up and throwing them in the air. Viewers all along the East Coast could hear Rayburn shouting on live TV, "Get those goddamn pigeons out of here."

Truman, who was a huge underdog to Dewey in the election, finally took the podium and gave a rousing speech. In the view of veteran New

York Times media critic Jack Gould, this was the moment that TV political coverage came of age.

FIGURE 7 HARRY TRUMAN

"If there had been any doubt that television was going to place an increasing premium on personality in politics, it was removed by the appearance of President Truman shortly after 2 a.m. on Thursday," Gould wrote.

"Appearing in a white suit and a dark tie, which perhaps is the best masculine garb for the video cameras, the president's performance was probably his most impressive since assuming office."

Nationwide TV coverage began at the 1952 conventions and has continued ever since.

# CHAPTER SIX:

# THE FIRST PRESIDENTIAL CAMPAIGN WITH WOMEN

By Ronald G. Shafer
*This column was published in the Washington Post on Aug. 5, 2020*

In the fall of 1840, eight decades before women won the right to vote, Elizabeth Clarkson climbed on her horse and led 400 women on horseback from Brookville, Ind., to a rally 75 miles away for presidential candidate William Henry "Old Tippecanoe" Harrison. At another meeting of 5,000 men, "Mother Clarkson" delivered a pro-Harrison speech while holding her infant son on one hip.

It marked the first time American women became openly involved in a presidential campaign, with Clarkson and her followers, backing the Whig Party ticket of Harrison and John Tyler against Democratic President Martin Van Buren.

In 1840, the idea of women taking part in the blood sport of politics was shocking to some men.

"Ladies are better mending their stockings or making puddings than becoming politicians," scolded the New York Herald.

That changed when the Whig Party decided to encourage female participation in the presidential campaign for "Tippecanoe and Tyler Too." Not that women could vote, of course. Who could imagine such a thing? But they could influence their husbands or boyfriends who would be casting ballots.

Some single Whig women teased their suitors that they wouldn't marry a man who wouldn't vote for Gen. Harrison, a hero of the War of 1812. In Tennessee, young women wore sashes embroidered with the words "WHIG HUSBANDS OR NONE." Some even carried out the threat. In Bristol, Maine, a young woman told her fiance, a local fisherman, that their wedding was off unless he agreed to vote for the Whig ticket. The young man swung to the Whigs, the

Providence Journal reported

FIGURE 8 WILLIAM HENRY HARRISON

Whig organizers sent "To the Ladies" invitations for wives to join their husbands at the big parades for Harrison's campaign. The Whigs brought wagonloads of women to rallies. In Bennington, Vt., it took 25 horses to pull one wagon filled with more than 100 women, the Harrison campaign newspaper reported.

The Whigs handed out handkerchiefs for women to wave, partly to draw the attention of the press. At a parade in Baltimore, windows were crowded with women who looked "with delight upon the scene to which their own presence with waving handkerchiefs and fluttering veils give a bright adornment," the Baltimore American reported. One woman reached out of a window and waved a bright red petticoat.

While marching in a Harrison rally in New York City, former New York mayor Philip Hone was struck by the flood of femininity along the route.

"The balconies and windows were filled with women, well-dressed, with bright eyes and bounding bosoms, waving handkerchiefs, exhibiting flags and garlands, and casting bouquets of flowers upon us," Hone wrote in his diary.

FIGURE 9 WHIG HANDKERCHIEF

Women did more than wave hankies. Some, like Clarkson, gave speeches for Harrison. In Seneca Falls, N.Y., 22-year-old Amelia Bloomer helped her new husband, Dexter Bloomer, edit his pro-Whig newspaper, the Seneca Falls County Courier. In Springfield, Ill., 21-year-old Mary Todd attended local Whig meetings; she also began dating 31-year-old Abraham Lincoln, who gave campaign speeches for Harrison. They would marry in 1842.

While sitting in a train car in Baltimore in 1840, British writer James Silk Buckingham was shocked to see something he had never witnessed while touring the United States. A well-dressed woman, "with gay bonnet, veil and shawl," walked down the aisle and began handing out copies of a political pamphlet.

"It is a good Harrison paper," she explained.

"My first impression was that the woman was insane," Buckingham wrote.

The woman was Lucy Kenney, the first woman to write political pamphlets for a presidential campaign.

The "Lowell Mill girls" who worked in textile mills in Lowell, Mass., actively supported Harrison as a champion of the working poor. They typically earned $2 a week working from 5 a.m. to 7 p.m. six days a week. Harriet Jane Hanson Robinson, who worked at one factory at age 15, later wrote that the women promoted Harrison "to show how wide-awake and up to date" they were.

"Harrison Women" were everywhere. They invaded the all-male Tippecanoe Clubs. They dubbed their bonnets "Tippecanoe Hats." They sewed banners to be carried in the big parades. They cooked food for the big gatherings.

"Women are the very life and soul of these movements of the People," proclaimed the Cincinnati Gazette.

Van Buren supporters frowned on these female intruders.

"We have been pained to see our fair countrywomen unsex themselves and stepping across the threshold to mingle in the fight," chided the North Carolina Standard.

When a wagonload of 50 women rolled by a saloon in a Whig parade in Buffalo, men pelted them with eggs. In a parade in Indianapolis, several women rode in a large canoe on wheels, setting off fistfights among some men in the crowd.

Van Buren's vice president, Richard Mentor Johnson, gave the Democratic view on the role of women. The rights of a woman, he said, were secured through the "coarser sex," her husband and brothers. "She does not appear at the polls to vote because she is privileged to be represented there by man."

Old Tippecanoe swept to victory in the election. He died after just one month in office, but "petticoat power" kept going. Many Harrison women attended the 1848 Seneca Falls Convention for women's rights, which, Amelia Bloomer wrote, marked the first time that women called for "the right to vote and hold office."

The next year, Bloomer began publishing "The Lily," a magazine that promoted temperance, abolition and female equality. She also promoted a new women's clothing item that gave her lasting fame: a loosefitting pantaloon that became known as "bloomers."

FIGURE 10 BLOOMERS

# CHAPTER SEVEN

# THE UGLIEST PRESIDENTIAL ELECTION IN HISTORY

By Ronald G. Shafer
*This column was published in the Washington Post on Nov.24, 2020*

About midnight on his way home from a play in New York City on Election Day in 1876, Daniel Sickles stopped by Republican national headquarters at the Fifth Avenue Hotel. The place was nearly deserted. GOP presidential candidate Rutherford B. Hayes was losing so badly that the party chairman had gone to bed with a bottle of whiskey.

Sickles, a former Union general, noticed something about the early returns, which gave Democratic New York Gov. Samuel J. Tilden a large lead. If four states where the results already were in dispute went to Hayes, he would win by one electoral vote.

Sickles sent telegrams under the name of the sleeping party chairman to Republican leaders in the four contested states urging them to safeguard votes for Hayes. "With your state sure for Hayes, he is elected. Hold your state."

Thus began the longest fought and closest presidential election in U.S. history. Much as President Trump is doing now, backers of Hayes, the governor of Ohio, charged the election was being stolen. The difference was that, unlike now, there was clear evidence of fraud and voter intimidation. The outcome in the tense, post-Civil War atmosphere not only decided a presidency but also led to nearly a century of racial segregation in the South.

The next day, Democratic newspapers trumpeted a Tilden victory. "GLORY! Tilden Triumphant," the Buffalo Courier headline said. A "Solid South Buries Sectional Hate," blared the Kansas City Times.

But the Republican New York Times — citing disputed results in Florida, Louisiana, South Carolina and Oregon — declared, "The Results Still Uncertain."

Back in Ohio, Hayes was pessimistic. "I think we are defeated in spite of the recent good news," he said.

As the days passed, the uncertainty increased. Tilden led by more than 250,000 votes in the popular vote in the 38 states. But he was one vote short of the 185 electoral votes needed for victory. Hayes had 165 votes.

All eyes focused on charges of intimidation of Black Republican voters in the three disputed Southern states (In Oregon, the issue was a disputed elector). Southern Whites were rebelling against Black political power granted under Reconstruction. Republican President Ulysses S. Grant had already sent federal troops to the states to help keep the peace.

FIGURE 11 SAMUEL TILDEN

In South Carolina, a majority Black state, armed White men belonging to "rifle clubs" and dressed in red shirts had harassed Republicans.

The "Red Shirts" killed six Black men in the Hamburg, S.C. massacre. The paramilitary group backed a former Confederate general for governor and threatened to kill Republican Gov. Daniel Chamberlain.

On Election Day in Edgefield, S.C., more than 300 armed Red Shirts on horseback "packed their horses so closely together that the only approach to the windows, back of which was the ballot box, was under the bellies of the beasts," the Times said. In Barnwell County, one newspaper reported there were "riflemen wearing red shirts, riding to and fro, cursing and threatening the negroes."

FIGURE 12 RUTHERFORD B. HAYES

Voter intimidation also was rampant in Louisiana and Florida. Vote fraud was widespread on both sides. According to the Rutherford B. Hayes Library, the Democrats used "repeaters," who voted repeatedly. They printed fraudulent ballots to trick illiterate Black voters into voting for Democrats. The national voter turnout was 81.8 percent, still the highest for a presidential election. But the number clearly was inflated. In South Carolina, despite voter suppression, the official turnout was 101 percent of eligible voters.

Republicans contended Hayes would have won easily with honest voting. A leading advocate was "Devil Dan" Sickles, who had campaigned for Hayes, a fellow Union general. Sickles had gained infamy in 1859 when, as a first-term congressman, he shot and killed his wife's lover — the son of "Star-Spangled Banner" author Francis Scott Key — in broad daylight in the park across the street from the White House. Sickles became the first accused murderer acquitted because of temporary insanity.

On Dec. 5, 1876, all of the states sent their official results to Washington to be counted and then announced by the president of the Senate. In the four contested states, Republican and Democratic officials filed separate tallies for Hayes or Tilden, throwing the election into chaos.

As now, Republicans controlled the Senate, and Democrats controlled the House. Finally in late January, Congress created a 15-member Electoral Commission of five senators, five House members and five Supreme Court justices. The commission voted separately on the four disputed states. They awarded all of the states — a total of 20 electoral votes — to Hayes by an 8-to-7 vote.

Now, Democrats charged the election was being stolen from Tilden. House Democrats began a filibuster. Amid cries of "Tilden or blood," one Washington newspaper reported on plans "to send a threatening and bellicose mob to the National Capital to see that the count is made according to their wishes."

Then on March 2 — nearly four months after the election and just two days before Inauguration Day — Congress reached agreement. After heated debate, at 4:10 a.m. the president of the Senate formally announced that Hayes had been elected the 19th president by an electoral college vote of 185 to 184.

On March 3, Grant hosted Hayes at the White House, where he was sworn in as president by the chief justice. On March 5, there was a public inauguration ceremony.

Tilden continued to maintain "the country knows that I was legally elected president." Dissidents dubbed Hayes "His Fraudulency."

Historians differ on what ended the standoff. Many believe Republicans made a deal to appease Southern Democrats in a secret meeting at Washington's Wormley's Hotel, which was owned by African American James Wormley. In his inauguration speech, Hayes said the time had come to allow the Southern states to govern themselves again. He soon withdrew federal troops from the South.

The rights of Black citizens in the South were devastated as a result. White rule soon prevailed, ushering in Jim Crow laws and segregation.

Thirty years later on the Senate floor, South Carolina's Benjamin "Pitchfork Ben" Tillman, a leader of the Red Shirts, boasted about the vote frauds of 1876.

"We set up the Democratic Party with one plank only, that this is the White man's country, and White men must govern it," Tillman said. "Under that banner, we went to battle. It was then that we shot them. It was then that we killed them. It was then that 'we stuffed ballot boxes,' because this disease needed a strong remedy."

Tillman added: "I do not ask anybody to apologize for it. I am only explaining why we did it."

# CHAPTER EIGHT

## THE "MISSISSIPPI PLAN" AND VOTER SUPPRESSION

By Ronald G. Shafer
*This column was published in the Washington Post on May 1, 2021*

On a hot August day in 1890, delegates gathered at Mississippi's Capitol Building in Jackson to begin work on a new state constitution. The overriding topic was the "suffrage question."

The convention's president, Solomon Saladin Calhoon, a White county judge, put the voting issue bluntly. "Let's tell the truth if it bursts the bottom of the universe," he said. "We came here to exclude the Negro. Nothing short of this will answer."

Delegates eventually adopted a literacy test and a poll tax geared to suppress the Black vote in a state with a Black majority. The "Mississippi Plan" became the model throughout the South, part of a raft of racially oppressive Jim Crow laws that ended Reconstruction.

President Joe Biden and others warn that Jim Crow-style disenfranchisement is resurfacing in efforts by Republican legislatures in Georgia, Texas and other states to restrict voting. The moves are in response to former President Donald Trump's false claims of widespread voter fraud in the 2020 presidential election. Republican Gov. Brian Kemp denies Georgia's new law is discriminatory, but many will disproportionately affect areas where large turnouts by African American voters in 2020 helped Biden and two Democratic senators win.

Mississippi's 1890 convention sought to find a way around the 15th Amendment to the Constitution, which gave African Americans the vote.

Just two decades earlier, the Mississippi state legislature had made history by electing Hiram Revels to the U.S. Senate. He was the first African American member to serve in either house of Congress. But that moment of racial progress quickly vanished.

After President Rutherford B. Hayes removed all federal troops from Southern states in 1877, White Democrats who'd supported slavery and the Confederacy began regaining control of the states from Black and White Republicans.

Nearly all of the Mississippi convention's 134 delegates were White Democrats with one African American Republican. A White Republican named Marsh Cook had campaigned for a seat vowing to protect the rights of Black voters. A few weeks before the convention, his bullet-riddled body was found on a rural road.

The Jackson Clarion-Ledger lamented the murder but added "those who did it felt they were doing their country a service in removing a man who had become so offensive."

At the convention, one delegate candidly summarized the dilemma of White Democrats: "It is no secret that there has not been a full vote and a fair count in Mississippi since 1875 – that in plain words, we have been stuffing ballot boxes, committing perjury…carrying the elections by fraud and violence."

He suggested a way to weed out "unqualified" voters, proposing to require that a voter "must read and write the English language or he is debarred from the privilege of voting." Most of the state's African Americans were former slaves who had been denied an education.

Men who can't read "are not of character to entrust the ballot," the Clarion-Ledger agreed. "A plan of this kind would disenfranchise few White people, denying the ballot only to the idle and thriftless class."

The convention adopted a provision that a qualified voter must "be able to read any section" of the state constitution, or "shall be able to understand the same when read to him." A voter also could be questioned to determine his literacy.

Delegates rightly foresaw that White registrars would ask White voters simple questions, while demanding that African Americans answer complex queries. In the following years Black voters in the state were asked such things as "How many bubbles are in a bar of soap?"

FIGURE 13 MISSISSIPPI SEN. BLANCH KELSO BRUCE,

The convention also adopted a $2 poll tax (equal to about $58 today) that disproportionately eliminated Black voters, most of whom were very poor.

The only African American delegate, Isaiah Montgomery, supported these requirements. He had been enslaved by the brother of Confederate president Jefferson Davis of Mississippi. Montgomery, an educated and successful businessman, said that Mississippi's uneducated Blacks would approve of the restrictions for the good of the state.

Montgomery's optimistic view was that African Americans would be treated equally as their education level rose. "The two great races shall peaceably travel side by side, each mutually assisting the other to mount higher," he declared in a nationally publicized speech at the convention.

Revered Black abolitionist Frederick Douglass said Montgomery "commits unconscionable treason to his race in surrendering his franchise."

Earlier African Americans from 40 counties in Mississippi had protested to President Benjamin Harrison, but he declined to intervene.

The convention adopted the constitution on Nov. 1, 1890, adding the new requirements to a provision allowing voting by male residents age 21 and older "except idiots, insane persons and Indians not taxed."

When northern newspapers denounced the literacy test as discriminatory, one Mississippi state senator responded: "I deny that the educational test was intended to exclude Negroes from voting...the sole purpose was to exclude persons of both races who from want of intelligence are unsafe depositors of political power. That more Negroes would be excluded is true...but that is not our fault."

That rationale was rejected a decade later by James Vardaman, the white supremacist who became governor of Mississippi in 1903. "There is no use to equivocate or lie about the matter," Vardaman said. "Mississippi's constitutional convention of 1890 was held for no other purpose than to eliminate the [n-word] from politics. Not the 'ignorant and vicious' as some of the apologists would have you believe."

The new law took effect in the 1892 election with a dramatic impact. Only 8,615 of the state's 76,742 Black voters qualified to cast a ballot. Soon the Mississippi approach spread to other Southern states. It remained in place for nearly 70 years until Congress passed the Voting Rights Act of 1965.

In his speech to Congress proposing the law, President Lyndon B. Johnson specifically singled out the need to eliminate literacy tests. For a Southern Black voter, he said, "even a college degree cannot be used to prove that he can read or write."

Johnson declared: "We cannot, we must not, refuse to protect the right of every American to vote in every election that he may desire to participate in."

# CHAPTER NINE

# WHY A VEEP CAN'T DECIDE A PRESIDENTIAL ELECTION

By Ronald G. Shafer

Jan. 6, 2021
*(This online story about events of 1857 was published
early on the morning of Jan. 6 and updated throughout
the day to reflect current breaking news about the
attack on the U.S. Capitol by Trump supporters.)*

Even if he wanted to, Vice President Mike Pence can't on his own declare President Trump the winner of the 2020 presidential election when he announces the electoral vote count at a joint session of Congress — thanks, in part, to a snowstorm in Wisconsin in late 1856.

At the presidential count ceremony in 1857 a dispute erupted over Wisconsin's five electoral votes, which had been delivered a day after the deadline because of a blizzard. The dispute didn't affect the election of Democrat James Buchanan as president. But Congress decided to take actions that might keep future elections from being hijacked.

The precedent of 1857 led to procedures that are in place for Wednesday's congressional certification of the election. Regardless of growing Republican efforts to disrupt the ceremony, the electoral votes will be counted out loud to certify the election of Joe Biden as President and Kamala D. Harris as vice president.

Still refusing to concede the election, Trump is falsely suggesting the ceremony is a last-minute chance for congressional Republicans to reverse the election.

On Wednesday, at an election protest on the Ellipse, Trump urged Pence "to do the right thing" by giving states the right to "recertify" the election. The crowd roared in agreement, chanting, "Send it back!"

Not long afterward, Pence released a letter making it clear he could not intervene. "My oath to support and defend the Constitution constrains me from claiming unilateral authority to determine which electoral votes should be counted and which should not," Pence wrote. "My role as presiding officer is largely ceremonial."

The 12th Amendment of the U.S. Constitution requires that the president of the Senate — the vice president — "shall, in the presence of the Senate and House of Representatives, open all the certificates and the votes shall then be counted."

So every four years in the first week of January, House and Senate members assemble in the House chambers for a joint session of Congress. Pages carry in two mahogany wood boxes filled with the sealed envelopes of certified electoral votes from the 50 states and the District of Columbia.

The vice president pulls out each envelope and hands it to one of four lawmakers designated as "tellers" who tally the vote. The vice president announces the final count, so Pence will announce the defeat of the Trump-Pence ticket.

Usually this ceremony is simply ceremonial. That's the way the one on Feb. 11, 1857, started out — back when the presidential inauguration wasn't until March 4.

"At an early hour the galleries and lobbies were crowded with eager spectators, awaiting the opening of a ceremony imposing alike for its simplicity and for the dignified formalities which attend the final consummation of a Presidential election," the Washington Intelligencer reported.

At 12:20 p.m. the doors of the House chamber were thrown open and in trooped the U.S. senators as House members stood. Senate President Pro Tempore James Mason, a Virginia Democrat and a grandson of Founding Father George Mason, served as the presiding officer because the vice president, William King, had died six weeks after being sworn in and had never been replaced.

Mason proceeded with the traditional drawing of the votes. But when he announced Wisconsin's votes for Republican John Fremont, Rep. John Letcher (D-Va.) jumped up and objected that the Wisconsin tallies were illegal because they had been filed in the state capital of Madison one day after the required deadline.

Mason didn't know what to do; he ruled Letcher's objection out of order and finished the count including the Wisconsin votes. The final result was 174 electoral votes for Buchanan, 114 for Fremont and eight for Millard Fillmore of the Know-Nothing Party.

Kentucky's Sen. John Crittenden, a member of the Know-Nothing Party, demanded to know if by accepting Wisconsin's vote, Mason was assuming "the privilege of determining a presidential election and saying who shall be President? I protest against any such power."

Sen. Andrew Butler (D-S.C.) chimed in that such use of "arbitrary power could make a president of the United States without an election."

The Wisconsin votes didn't make any difference in the outcome of the 1856 election. But some lawmakers warned that permitting the presiding officer to accept a state's illegal vote could set a "dangerous precedent," according to Congress's record of the debate in the Congressional Globe.

"Suppose the result of the election would depend on the vote of that state," said Rep. James Orr (D-S.C.).

If anybody was going to decide if votes were valid, it should be Congress, argued Sen. Robert Toombs (D-Ga.).

"I do not consider that the Presiding Officer has a right to close the mouths of Senators and Representatives here, in whose hands the decision of this question must rest," Toombs said.

Mason protested that he was just doing his job. "Much confusion prevailed" with "half a dozen gentlemen striving at the same time for the floor," the New York Times reported. At this point, the senators decided to return to the Senate chamber to hash out the issue. "I will trust no man to determine for me who shall be president of the United States in his arbitrary decision," Butler told his colleagues. Suppose the presiding vice president had to consider two opposing electoral vote totals from the same state, wouldn't he be inclined to go with votes for the candidate of his own political party?

"I assure you, sir," Butler said. "It is a power which in the time of temptation — and God knows when the time of temptation may arrive for someone to desire to be President to rule in this country — I would not like to trust too many people."

The discussions went into the next day. Then the Senate returned to the House, and eventually a compromise was agreed on. Wisconsin's votes were counted because Congress had agreed that an "Act of God" had prevented the electors from reaching the state capital of Madison on time.

The process created a sort of unwritten precedent if reforms were made. Cries for reform escalated after the 1876 presidential race between Republican Rutherford B. Hayes and Democrat Samuel Tilden. Three Southern states filed opposing elector slates. Congress had to create an Electoral Commission that in 1877 by a party-line vote gave the presidency to Hayes over Tilden, who had 200,000 more votes.

The fears raised in 1857 were "prophetic of the issue to arise in 1877," a Richmond newspaper noted in 1887, because they raised fears about challenging votes in a close election. That year Congress finally passed the Electoral Count Act of 1887.

FIGURE 14 PRESIDENTIAL CERTIFICATION

The official name of the measure was: "An act to fix the day for the meeting of the electors of President and Vice-President, and to provide for and regulate the counting of the votes for President and Vice-President, and the decision of questions arising thereon." As the title suggests, the act is downright confusing. One observer called it "unintelligible." But the 809-word act became the framework for the presidential electoral count that Congress uses now.

Following the precedents of 1857, the act bars the vice president from arbitrarily deciding to reject state votes. If there are any valid objections, the House and Senate withdraw to confer separately. Objections must be stated in writing in advance and signed by at least one member of both the House and Senate.

The requirements hardly ever come up. The last time was 2005 when several Democrats unsuccessfully challenged Ohio's electoral votes for George W. Bush.

Now some pro-Trump lawmakers vow that they will seek to block the certification of Biden's victory. The effort is all but certain to meet the same fate as the one in 2005: failure.

# CHAPTER TEN

# THE VICE PRESIDENT'S ENSLAVED WIFE

By Ronald G. Shafer
*This column was published in the Washington Post on Feb. 7, 2021*

She was born enslaved and remained that way her entire life, even after she became Richard Mentor Johnson's "bride."

Johnson, a Kentucky congressman who eventually became the nation's ninth vice president in 1837, couldn't legally marry Julia Chinn. Instead the couple exchanged vows at a local church with a wedding celebration organized by the enslaved people at his family's plantation in Great Crossing, according to Miriam Biskin, who wrote about Chinn decades ago. Chinn died nearly four years before Johnson took office. But because of controversy over her, Johnson is the only vice president in American history who failed to receive enough electoral votes to be elected. The Senate voted him into office.

The couple's story is complicated and fraught, historians say. As an enslaved woman, Chinn could not consent to a relationship, and there's no record of how she regarded him. Though she wrote to Johnson during his lengthy absences from Kentucky, the letters didn't survive.

Amrita Chakrabarti Myers, who is working on a book about Chinn, wrote about the hurdles in a blog post for the Association of Black Women Historians.

"While doing my research, I was struck by how Julia had been erased from the history books," wrote Myers, a history professor at Indiana University. "Nobody knew who she was. The truth is that Julia (and Richard) are both victims of legacies of enslavement, interracial sex, and silence around black women's histories."

Johnson's life is far better documented.

He was elected as a Democrat to the state legislature in 1802 and to Congress in 1806. The folksy, handsome Kentuckian gained a reputation as a champion of the common man.

Back home in Great Crossing, he fathered a child with a local seamstress, but didn't marry her when his parents objected, according to the biography "The Life and Times of Colonel Richard M. Johnson of Kentucky." Then, in about 1811, Johnson, 31, turned to Chinn, 21, who had been enslaved at Blue Spring Plantation since childhood.

Johnson called Chinn "my bride." His "great pleasure was to sit by the fireplace and listen to Julia as she played on the pianoforte," Biskin wrote in her account.

The couple soon had two daughters, Imogene and Adaline. Johnson gave his daughters his last name and openly raised them as his children.

Johnson became a national hero during the War of 1812. At the Battle of the Thames in Canada, he led a horseback attack on the British and their Native American allies. He was shot five times but kept fighting. During the battle, the Shawnee chief Tecumseh was killed.

In 1819, "Colonel Dick" was elected to the U.S. Senate. When he was away in Washington for long periods, he left Chinn in charge of the 2,000-acre plantation and told his White employees that they should "act with the same propriety as if I were home."

FIGURE 15 JULIA CHINN

Chinn's status was unique. While enslaved women wore simple cotton dresses, Chinn's wardrobe "included fancy dresses that turned heads when Richard hosted parties," Christina Snyder wrote in her book, "Great Crossings: Indians, Settlers & Slaves in the Age of Jackson." In 1825, Chinn and Johnson hosted the Marquis de Lafayette during his return to America.

In the mid-1820s, Johnson opened on his plantation the Choctaw Academy, a federally funded boarding school for Native Americans. He hired a local Baptist minister as director. Chinn ran the academy's medical ward.

"Julia is as good as one half the physicians, where the complaint is not dangerous," Johnson wrote in a letter. He paid the academy's director extra to educate their daughters "for a future as free women."

Johnson tried to advance his daughters in local society, and both would later marry White men. But when he spoke at a local July Fourth celebration, the Lexington Observer reported, prominent White citizens wouldn't let Adaline sit with them in the pavilion. Johnson sent his daughter to his carriage, rushed through his speech and then angrily drove away.

When Johnson's father died, he willed ownership of Chinn to his son. He never freed his common-law wife.

"Whatever power Chinn had was dependent on the will and the whims of a White man who legally owned her," Snyder wrote. Then, in 1833, Chinn died of cholera. It's unclear where she is buried.

Johnson went on to even greater national prominence. In 1836, President Andrew Jackson backed Vice President Martin Van Buren as his successor. At Jackson's urging, Van Buren — a fancy dresser who had never fought in war — picked war hero Johnson as his running mate. Nobody knew how the Shawnees' chief was slain in the War of 1812, but Johnson's campaign slogan was, "Rumpsey, Dumpsey. Johnson Killed Tecumseh."

FIGURE 16 RICHARD MENTOR JOHNSON

Johnson's relationship with Chinn became a campaign issue. Southern newspapers denounced him as "the great Amalgamationist." A mocking cartoon showed a distraught Johnson with a hand over his face bewailing "the scurrilous attacks on the Mother of my Children."

Van Buren won the election, but Johnson's 147 electoral votes were one short of what he needed to be elected. Virginia's electors refused to vote for him. It was the only time Congress chose a vice president.

When Van Buren ran for reelection in 1840, Democrats declined to nominate Johnson at their Baltimore convention. It is the only time a party didn't pick any vice-presidential candidate. The spelling-challenged Jackson warned that Johnson would be a "dead wait" on the ticket.

"Old Dick" still ended up being the leading choice and campaigned around the country wearing his trademark red vest. But Van Buren lost to Johnson's former commanding officer, Gen. William Henry Harrison.

Johnson never remarried, but he reportedly had sexual relationships with other enslaved women who couldn't consent to them. The former vice president won a final election to the Kentucky legislature in 1850 but died a short time later at the age of 70.

His brothers laid claim to his estate at the expense of his surviving daughter, Imogene, who was married to a White man named Daniel Pence.

"At some point in the early twentieth century," Myers wrote, "perhaps because of heightened fears of racism during the Jim Crow era, members of Imogene Johnson Pence's line, already living as white people, chose to stop telling their children that they were descended from Richard Mentor Johnson ... and his black wife. It wasn't until the late 20th century that younger Pences, by then already in their 40s, 50s, and 60s, began discovering the truth of their heritage."

# CHAPTER ELEVEN

# THE FIRST PRESIDENTIAL IMPEACHMENT TRY AND TYLER TOO

By Ronald G. Shafer
*This column was published in the Washington Post on Sept. 23, 2019*

On July 22, 1842, Virginia Rep. John Minor Botts rose from his seat in the House of Representatives to introduce the first proposal in U.S. history to impeach a president. The president was fellow Whig John Tyler. Botts vowed to "head him or die."

Whig Party leader Henry Clay of Kentucky cautioned that impeachment might be a risky way to counter the president's bitter clashes with the Whig-controlled Congress.

"There is cause enough, God knows," Clay said, "but it is a novel proceeding, full of important consequences, present and future, and should not be commenced but upon full consideration."

Some of the rhetoric aimed at Tyler echoes what House Democrats are leveling at President Trump. House Intelligence Committee Chairman Adam B. Schiff said allegations that Trump pressured Ukraine to investigate Joe Biden's son may make impeachment inevitable. House Speaker Nancy Pelosi also sent a letter to Republicans and Democrats that demanded more information from the director of national intelligence about Trump's interactions with Ukraine but did not use the I-word.

When John Tyler faced impeachment 177 years ago, it was the Whigs who decided to create an investigative committee headed by a respected elder statesman, former president John Quincy Adams, who had become a Massachusetts congressman.

The 51-year-old Tyler, a former Democratic U.S. senator from Virginia, had only recently switched to the Whig Party. As president, he began vetoing so many bills passed by Congress that the Whigs kicked him out of their party. Mobs of angry Whigs protested in front of the White House.

The anger boiled over on the House floor, where Rep. Edward Stanly of North Carolina got into a fistfight with Tyler's best friend, Rep. Henry Wise of Virginia. Stanly complained of Tyler: "He lies like a dog."

The president was aware of the discontent in Congress. He wrote a friend, "I am told that one of the madcaps talks of impeachment." That "madcap" was Botts, who on July 11 gave notice of his plans, warning, "If the power of impeachment is not exercised by the House in less than six months, ten thousand bayonets will gleam on Pennsylvania Avenue."

Eleven days later, Botts formally introduced a petition to impeach Tyler "on the grounds of his ignorance of the interest and true policy of this government and want of qualification for the discharge of the important duties of President of the United States." The House voted to table the proposal for the time being.

Botts separately specified his charges against Tyler. Among them: "I charge him with the high crime and misdemeanor of endeavoring to excite a disorganizing and revolutionary spirit in the country, by inviting a disregard of, and disobedience to a law of Congress." He charged the president with "abuse of the veto power, to gratify his personal and political resentment," and of being "utterly unworthy and unfit to have the destinies of this nation in his hands as chief magistrate."

FIGURE 17 JOHN TYLER

The same Democratic newspapers that had pilloried the Whig presidential ticket of "Tippecanoe and Tyler Too" defended Tyler and attacked Botts. "The bastard son of Virginia has performed his foolish threat and produced articles of impeachment against the President of the United States," wrote the Madisonian.

Clay, who had resigned from the Senate to prepare to run for president in 1844, feared a voter backlash to a premature impeachment action. "Let [Tyler] serve out his time and go back to Virginia from whence the Whigs have bitter cause to lament that they ever sent him forth," he said.

Botts rejected such concerns.

"There may be some honest but timid men" who fear impeachment efforts would create sympathy for the president, he said. "But to my mind it would be quite as reasonable to suffer a mad dog to escape that runs through the public streets biting every living thing he met with, from an apprehension that it might excite a sympathy for him by the cry of kill him."

The Whigs were especially frustrated because Congress had failed to override any of Tyler's vetoes. The clash hit a breaking point on Aug. 9 when Tyler vetoed a major tariff bill. Adams took to the House floor to declare that the president had put the legislative and executive branches "in a state of civil war."

On Aug. 11, the House authorized a 13-member Select Committee on the Veto headed by Adams to investigate the president's actions. Adams despised Tyler because he was a slaveholder.

The committee reported back just a week later. The majority report accused Tyler of "gross abuse of constitutional power and bold assumptions of powers never vested in him by any law" and of having assumed "the whole legislative power to himself." The report said Tyler had "strangled" the life out of Congress and committed "offenses of the gravest character." The majority also charged Tyler with obstruction of justice by withholding information needed to investigate the "misdeeds by government."

The majority concluded "the case has occurred" that was "contemplated by the founders of the Constitution by the grant of the power to impeach the President of the United States." However, the report didn't recommend proceeding with impeachment because "of the present state of public affairs."

With the nation sharply divided, the report said, such action would "prove abortive." The House approved the majority report. Tyler responded that he had "been accused without evidence and condemned without a hearing." In a letter to a friend, the president said he apparently had committed the high crime of "sustaining the Constitution of the country and daring to have an opinion of my own."

On Jan. 10, 1843, the House voted on Botts's articles of impeachment. But the Whigs had lost control of the body in the 1842 election, and the resolution failed. Tyler eventually issued a total of 10 vetoes (far below Franklin D. Roosevelt's record 635 vetoes).

The Whigs finally got some revenge in Tyler's final month in office, March 1845, when Congress overrode a veto of a bill on building Marine service ships. Thus, Tyler became the first U.S. president to have a veto overridden.

# CHAPTER TWELVE

# BARRICADED IN HIS OFFICE

By Ronald G. Shafer
*This column was published in the Washington Post on Jan 26, 2021*

When Andrew Johnson illegally tried to fire War Secretary Edwin Stanton in 1868, the president's congressional foes saw their chance to impeach him. But Stanton had to hold his post to keep the issue alive.

A lawmaker sent Stanton a one-word telegram: "Stick."

The House impeached Johnson in three days in late February. Meanwhile, Stanton camped out in his War Department office and thwarted attempts to replace him. Johnson's Senate trial lasted into May.

In 2021, it took two days for the House to impeach President Donald Trump for the second time for his role in inciting his supporters to attack the U.S. Capitol on Jan. 6. The former president's Senate trial is set to begin Feb. 9.

Trump will spend the trial at Mar-a-Lago, his luxurious private club in Florida. In 1868, to the chagrin of his wife, Stanton barricaded himself in his office and slept on a couch for more than two months until Johnson's trial ended.

Stanton is mostly remembered as the man who said "Now he belongs to the ages" when Abraham Lincoln died after being shot at Ford's Theatre on April 14, 1865. Johnson, the Democratic vice president, succeeded Lincoln, a Republican. Stanton stayed on as war secretary.

The new president and Stanton clashed over post-Civil War policies. Stanton and the Radical Republican faction in Congress backed Lincoln's reconstruction plan to advance the rights of Black people in the South. Johnson, a racist from Tennessee, pushed to ease sanctions on former Confederates.

Finally, on Feb. 21, 1868, Johnson fired Stanton and appointed an interim war secretary. That night, the 53-year-old Stanton slept on the sofa in his second-floor office a half-block from the White House. The next morning, several House Republicans joined him for breakfast.

That same day, House Republicans began moving to impeach Johnson for violating the Tenure of Office Act, which barred the dismissal of federal appointees without Congress's approval.

Meanwhile, Stanton, who was a lawyer, had obtained a warrant for the arrest of his designated replacement, Gen. Lorenzo Thomas, for his role in violating the act. A U.S. marshal arrested the general at his home early on Feb. 22, while he was having breakfast and nursing a hangover.

Thomas got out on bail and went to the War Department shortly before noon to tell Stanton that he was taking over as interim war secretary. "Mr. Stanton replied that he could do no such thing," the Washington Star reported. The two men were old rivals, and Stanton poured glasses of whiskey as they talked.

At some point, Gen. Ulysses S. Grant, who headed the Army, came in. Grant joked to Stanton: "I am surprised to find you here. I supposed you would be at my headquarters for protection."

Stanton settled in. That evening he and an Army sergeant who stayed with him tried to boil an Irish stew in Stanton's fireplace. The stew burned and "stank up the office."

The next day, Ellen Stanton arrived by carriage. The couple quarreled over the secretary's decision to remain in his office. His wife wanted him to resign and drove off in a huff. She refused to send over food and fresh linen from home.

FIGURE 18 EDWIN STANTON

Stanton vowed to stay put until Johnson's Senate trial was over. His main complaint, friends said, was that "he wished the reporters would leave him alone."

The clash made headlines across the country. "The telegraph wires are laden with 'wars and rumor of wars' between the contending powers for the occupancy of the dirty, dingy room devoted to the secretary's use in the dirty, dingy building in Washington city," one news service reported.

Republicans accused Johnson of trying to stage a coup. The New York Herald warned, "If violence is used in ejecting Mr. Stanton, 100,000 men are ready to come to Washington to put him back in."

The House impeached Johnson on Feb. 24, and the Senate trial began March 2. Stanton dug in for a long wait.

He had barricades put up blocking "all the passages in the War Office. He has had heavy new shutters placed on the windows," the

New Orleans Times reported. "If the President should move against the stronghold, we advise him to employ a fire engine to wash its opponent out."

Grant doubled the guards outside Stanton's office door. The war secretary didn't dare "to go out of earshot of his office," the Boston Post reported. Some War Department officials said they would be duty bound to recognize Thomas as the new secretary if Stanton walked outside "even for a moment."

Rep. John Logan (R-Ill.), a former general, moved in as a kind of personal security guard and slept on a cot. Logan organized members of the Grand Army of the Republic, a fraternal group of Union veterans, to stand watch in the area. He offered to mobilize armed support, but Stanton said he didn't want any bloodshed on his behalf. (Logan Circle in Washington is named after him.)

At first Johnson and Thomas vowed to remove Stanton by force, but their empty threats soon drew ridicule. Newspapers mocked Thomas as "Lorenzo the Magnificent." The New York Herald reported sarcastically, "The President in a fit of rage had gone over personally and unceremoniously pitched [Stanton] out the window at the War office."

Stanton continued to operate as war secretary except for going to Cabinet meetings. Interim secretary Thomas "submits to Stanton's orders and is locked out, laughed at and treated with contempt," complained Johnson's Navy Secretary Gideon Welles.

Johnson gave up the idea of trying to root out Stanton, which could backfire at his impeachment trial. By April, Stanton was able to sneak home in an Army ambulance to sleep one night in his own bed. He and his wife made up, and another time they slipped away for a weekend in Baltimore.

On May 16, to the surprise of many, the Senate acquitted Johnson by one vote. The same day, Stanton "relinquished" his office, or as one newspaper put it: The war secretary "who could not be kicked out nor cuffed out, nor dragged out, nor reasoned out, nor shamed out of office, has accepted the impeachment notice to quit and has left."

Stanton went home and resumed his private law practice. Later that year, Grant was elected president. In late 1869, Grant appointed Stanton to the U.S. Supreme Court, but he never served. Four days after being confirmed by the Senate, he died of an asthma attack on Dec. 24.

Lincoln's son, Robert Todd Lincoln, wrote a letter of condolence to Stanton's son, Edwin Stanton Jr.

"When I recall the kindness of your father to me," he said, "when my father was lying dead, and I felt utterly desperate, hardly able to realize the truth, I am as little able to keep my eyes from filling with tears as he was then."

# CHAPTER THIRTEEN

## GUESS WHO'S NOT COMING TO THE INAUGURATION

By Ronald G. Shafer
*This column was published in the Washington Post on Jan. 8, 2021*

The peeved president decided to skip his successor's inauguration ceremony.

The year was 1869, and the president was Andrew Johnson, who detested incoming President Ulysses S. Grant. The feeling was mutual. Grant refused to ride in the same carriage with Johnson to the Capitol.

Now the country faces a much uglier transfer of power between President Trump, who falsely maintains the election was stolen from him, and Joe Biden.

On Thursday night, as calls grew for his removal from office in the wake of a violent attack on the U.S. Capitol by his supporters, Trump finally acknowledged there will be a new president on Jan. 20 and pledged a "smooth, orderly, seamless transition of power."

But on Friday morning, Trump tweeted that he would not attend Biden's inauguration, which would make him the first president to skip his successor's swearing-in since Johnson 152 years ago.

Johnson decided to be a no-show at Grant's inauguration at the last minute. The two men had clashed often after Republican President Abraham Lincoln was assassinated on April 14, 1865, and Vice

President Johnson, a Tennessee Democrat, became president. Johnson's racist views offended Grant, who headed the Army. Then Grant resisted Johnson's efforts to oust Secretary of War Edwin Stanton.

In February 1868, Johnson became the first president ever impeached by the House after he fired Stanton in violation of the Tenure of Office Act, which barred dismissing appointed officials without Congress's consent. Grant supported the impeachment. He and Johnson hotly accused each other of being liars. The Senate acquitted Johnson by one vote.

Johnson was so unpopular that the Democrats didn't nominate him for a second term in the 1868 election. The Republicans ran Grant, who won easily. Now the two old foes would be together for the transition.

The first sign of trouble surfaced in early January in news reports that Grant indicated "he will not occupy the same carriage with Mr. Johnson going to and from the Capitol." The inauguration committee came up with a compromise plan for the two men to ride in separate carriages. Johnson's carriage would go up the right side of Pennsylvania Avenue and Grant's up the left side.

Johnson didn't make a public response, but Grant's snub offended Navy Secretary Gideon Welles. At a Cabinet meeting in January 1869, Welles suggested to Johnson that he skip Grant's inauguration on March 4, because the president-elect was "so disrespectful and wanting in courtesy."

Welles noted Johnson wouldn't be the first president to miss his successor's inauguration. John Adams had stormed out of Washington at 4 a.m. the day of Thomas Jefferson's inauguration in 1801. His son President John Quincy Adams left Washington the day before the 1829 swearing in of Andrew Jackson, whom Adams despised.

FIGURE 19 ULYSSES S. GRANT

(Often overlooked is that President Martin Van Buren didn't attend the 1841 inauguration of William Henry Harrison, even though the two men were friendly. No one is sure why.)

Johnson warmed to Welles's suggestion. At the next Cabinet meeting, the president told Cabinet members, Welles wrote in his diary, that "we owed it to ourselves to take the ground that we could not, with proper self-respect, witness the inauguration of a man whom we knew to be untruthful, faithless and false."

Several Cabinet members, especially Secretary of State William Seward, wanted to go. Seward had served under Lincoln. The night John Wilkes Booth shot Lincoln at Ford's Theatre, a co-conspirator stabbed Seward nearly to death in his bed at home.

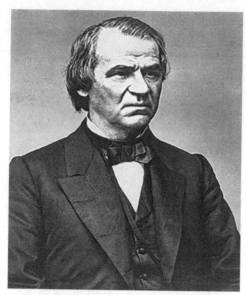

FIGURE 20 ANDREW JOHNSON

Treasury Secretary Hugh McCulloch also was "itching" to go and argued that by not going, Johnson would "look small," Welles wrote in his diary. Attorney General William Evarts urged that the president and Cabinet members go as a group.

To Welles's chagrin, at the March 2 Cabinet meeting, Johnson agreed that he and his Cabinet members should attend Grant's inauguration together. Welles complained "so we are likely to form part of the pageant — be a tail to the Grant kite." The plan was to gather at the White House on the morning of March 4.

Then Johnson changed his mind.

On a cold inauguration morning, Welles was the first to arrive at the White House. He wrote that he shook hands with Johnson, who "said quietly I think we will finish our work here without going to the Capitol."

The other Cabinet members began drifting in. McCulloch "was disappointed and disturbed" by Johnson's decision. Evarts was determined to change the president's mind and wouldn't take off his overcoat. Seward arrived last, smoking a cigar. He was unaware of what was going on. As Johnson worked at his desk, Seward "asked aloud if we would not be late, 'Ought we not start immediately?'" Welles wrote in his diary.

Johnson informed him that he was inclined to "finish out our work here." What nobody knew until later was that the president had sent Grant a letter the previous day suggesting that they ride together to the ceremony. Grant didn't reply.

The public knew nothing of all this. About a half-hour before the noon ceremony, Grant arrived in his open carriage at the White House where an empty carriage was waiting for Johnson. A crowd had gathered as soldiers of Dupont's light artillery battery stood at attention in front of the mansion.

One soldier was "waiting to fire the gun which was to be the signal to the whole city that President Johnson had entered his carriage," the New York Herald reported.

"A few minutes passed in silence, while all eyes were turned toward the lofty portal of the White House, eager to behold the appearance of the outgoing president. But they looked in vain," the Herald reported.

"Notice was given that the President was too much engaged to join the procession." The soldier fired his signal gun, and the procession headed toward the Capitol. The president's carriage was missing.

As his successor was about to be sworn in, Johnson stayed in the White House signing bills and, as some newspapers reported, "pardoning criminals." At noon, he stood up and shook hands with his Cabinet members. As he headed out the door for the last time, he said, "I fancy I can already smell the sweet mountain air of Tennessee."

Johnson backers supported the snub. "Whatever Andy Johnson was called — and that was pretty nearly everything — 'hypocrite' was not one of his names," one New York newspaper wrote.

Other papers, however, quoted a "Democratic contemporary" who lamented that Johnson's final act typified the actions of the impeached, one-term president.

"When his own personality rose to a conspicuous height, it almost invariably suffered from the impetuous disregard of surrounding circumstances; when he remembered only himself and became excited with a sense of wrong, he almost invariably forgot the dignity of his station."

FIGURE 21 GRANT LEAVING WILLARD HOTEL

# CHAPTER FOURTEEN

# A TURBULENT TRANSITION

By Ronald G. Shafer
*This column was published in the Washington Post on Nov. 9, 2020*

President Herbert Hoover had just lost the 1932 election by a landslide to Franklin D. Roosevelt. But during a testy transition, Hoover kept trying to pressure the president-elect into fighting the Great Depression by supporting the very policies he had campaigned against.

Roosevelt, who had promised Americans a "New Deal" to get the country back on its feet, said no deal to endorsing the Hoover program. "It's not my baby," the New York governor told reporters.

FIGURE 22 FDR AND HERBERT HOOVER

The transition between President Trump and President-elect Joseph Biden until Inauguration Day on Jan. 20 promises to be the most contentious since the 1933 handoff. Trump has refused to concede the election, and a key administration official is following his lead, refusing to sign a letter that would enable Biden's transition team to formally start working.

During the Great Depression, inaugurations weren't held until March 4, the date set in the early days of the Republic when transportation was difficult.

So Hoover was a lame duck for four months. During that time, "he tried to persuade Roosevelt to abandon the New Deal, which Hoover remained sure could only lead to catastrophe," wrote Eric Rauchway in his book "Winter War. Hoover, Roosevelt and First Clash Over the New Deal."

Just as Trump claims the country is turning the corner on the pandemic, Hoover insisted an economic recovery was underway. Yet unemployment was rising above 20 percent and banks were failing across the country. Meantime, Adolph Hitler was taking power in Germany.

At their first post-election, face-to-face meeting on Nov. 22 in the Red Room of the White House, Hoover was shocked to see the severe disability of Roosevelt, who walked with braces because of polio. Hoover, 58, opened the meeting with an hour-long lecture on international economic issues.

The president took the 50-year-old Roosevelt's friendly nods as agreement to his plan that they jointly form a foreign debt commission. Hoover later told an adviser he had been "educating a very ignorant" if "well-meaning young man."

To Hoover's dismay, the next day Roosevelt rejected the president's plan. Hoover should proceed on his own if he wished, Roosevelt said. Or as humorist Will Rogers put it: "It's your onion. You peel it until March 4."

In December, Hoover tried again. In an exchange of telegrams, he urged Roosevelt to join in appointing a delegation to a World Economic Conference in London. When Roosevelt resisted, Hoover dropped the idea and made the telegrams public.

"Governor Roosevelt considers it undesirable" to engage in joint efforts on the economy, a White House statement said. FDR responded that "it is a pity" that Hoover was suggesting that he opposed "cooperative action."

The growing impression was that the two men were "congenitally unable to understand each other or to go along on methods," wrote Arthur Krock of the New York Times.

Roosevelt, not wanting to look uncooperative, phoned Hoover in early January to set up another meeting. The president was wary and had a stenographer on his end of the call. "I suppose he will tell the press I called *him* up and invited *him* to come here," Hoover told aides.

The two men met again on Jan. 20. This time they managed to reach an agreement for talks with Britain about its war debts to the United States, but only after Roosevelt took office.

The long transition took a scary turn on Feb. 15. In Miami, an unemployed bricklayer fired shots at an open convertible where Roosevelt was seated next to Chicago Mayor Anton Cermak. A woman in the crowd hit the gunman's arm as he was shooting. The bullets struck Cermak, who died a few weeks later.

Hoover expressed relief that Roosevelt was uninjured even as he quickly resumed lobbying him. On Feb. 18, he had the Secret Service deliver a confidential, handwritten letter to Roosevelt at the Hotel Astor in New York.

In the letter, which misspelled FDR's name as "Roosvelt," Hoover warned of "a most critical situation," of "public alarm" about the economy, especially bank failures. Hoover asked Roosevelt to issue a statement promising such actions as a balanced budget, even if it meant raising taxes, to restore public confidence and ensure "resumption of our march to recovery."

Roosevelt considered the letter "cheeky" and didn't respond for 12 days. Finally, he wrote back that "mere statements" wouldn't accomplish anything.

Hoover privately called his successor a "madman." In the view of historian Rauchway, Hoover's strategy now was to show that "the foolish New Dealer had been given every chance to come to his senses"; when FDR failed, Hoover would be redeemed, "and the people would return him to the presidency."

The clash continued up to the day before inauguration. Hoover invited Roosevelt and his family to a ceremonial 4 p.m. tea at the White

House. FDR's top economic adviser, Raymond Moley, stayed back at the nearby Mayflower Hotel to take a nap.

When Roosevelt arrived, he found that Hoover had called in the treasury secretary and the head of the Federal Reserve for a separate private meeting. "For God's sake, get Ray," FDR said. Moley rushed over from the Mayflower.

The private meeting went badly. Eleanor Roosevelt later told several reporters that she had heard the conversation through an open door. Hoover asked her husband to support closing the nation's banks temporarily to head off panic withdrawals.

"Like hell I will!" Roosevelt responded. "If you haven't the guts to do it yourself, I'll wait until I'm president to do it."

As the social gathering broke up, Roosevelt told Hoover that he needn't feel obligated to make a return courtesy call. Hoover responded stiffly: "Mr. Roosevelt, when you are in Washington as long as I have been, you will understand that the president of the United States calls on nobody."

An angry FDR said his son James "wanted to punch him [Hoover] in the eye." That evening, Hoover kept phoning Roosevelt until past midnight to try to get his backing on the banks.

Inauguration Day was cool and damp. Hoover and Roosevelt shared a blanket while riding in an open car from the White House to the Capitol. FDR tried to make small talk, but Hoover mostly stared grimly ahead. Roosevelt finally just waved his silk top hat to the crowd lining Pennsylvania Avenue.

In his inauguration speech before 100,000 people, Roosevelt addressed the Depression with the famous words, "The only thing we have to fear is fear itself." The next day was a Sunday. On Monday, the new president announced the closing of the nation's banks for a four-day "bank holiday."

Meanwhile, the states had ratified the 20th Amendment to the U.S. Constitution — it was known as the "lame duck amendment" — changing Inauguration Day to Jan. 20. Roosevelt died in 1945 during his fourth term in office and never had to go through another presidential transition.

# CHAPTER FIFTEEN

# GROVER CLEVELAND RETURNS

By Ronald G. Shafer
*This column was published in the Washington Post on Dec. 28, 2020*

President Trump may never concede to Joe Biden as he continues to contest an election he lost. But he's already channeling Grover Cleveland, America's 22nd and 24th president — the only commander in chief ever elected to two nonconsecutive terms.

"We're trying to do another four years," Trump said at a White House Christmas party. "Otherwise, I'll see you in four years."

That sounds like Cleveland's young wife, Frances, after her husband lost the 1888 election. "I want to find everything just as it is now, when we come back again," she told the White House staff. "We are coming back four years from today."

Like Trump, Stephen Grover Cleveland lost reelection amid charges of voter fraud. Unlike the 2020 election, there actually was clear evidence of fraud in some states, especially Indiana.

And unlike Trump, Cleveland graciously conceded to his opponent, Sen. Benjamin Harrison of Indiana. What's more, Cleveland not only attended Harrison's inauguration on a rainy day, but even held an umbrella over the new president as he delivered his inauguration speech.

Cleveland had won the presidency in 1884 as a 47-year-old bachelor despite revelations that he had fathered a son out of wedlock. A popular cartoon showed Cleveland and a woman holding a baby who was saying: "Ma, Ma. Where's my Pa?" But he also was known as "Grover the Good" for his reform actions as the Democratic mayor of Buffalo and the governor of New York.

FIGURE 23 GROVER CLEVELAND

The president soon boosted his image by marrying 21-year-old Frances Folsom, the daughter of a late friend. Cleveland is the only president ever to be married in a White House ceremony. The Clevelands took up a summer residence in an area of Northwest Washington. Today that neighborhood is called Cleveland Park.

Meanwhile, Cleveland made political enemies by vetoing more than 400 bills sent to him by the Republican Congress. He pressed for low tariffs on imported goods, antagonizing businesspeople. Warned that his stance might hurt him in the next election, Cleveland retorted, "What is the use of being elected or reelected unless you stand for something?"

In 1888, Republicans nominated Harrison, a Civil War general and the grandson of President William Henry "Old Tippecanoe" Harrison. Cleveland gave only one campaign speech because he considered campaigning by a president to be undignified.

Harrison gave more than 80 speeches from the front porch of his Indianapolis home. On the street in front of his house, he re-created his grandfather's colorful 1840 "log cabin and hard cider" campaign parades.

With Levi Morton as his running mate, he also took a note from his grandfather's 1840 campaign slogan — "Tippecanoe and Tyler Too" — recasting it as "Tippecanoe and Morton Too."

When the results came in, Cleveland won the popular vote by more than 100,000 votes, but Harrison won the electoral college vote 233 to 157. Democrats initially questioned narrow losses in New York and Indiana. In Indiana, Republicans openly encouraged the use of voters, known as "floaters," who agreed to vote for a candidate for a price.

After a brief delay, the Democratic Party's national campaign chairman conceded the election. "Gen. Harrison is elected beyond a doubt," he said. "Not only would it be foolish but wrong to make any further claim of the success of the Democratic ticket."

Cleveland wrote a personal letter to Harrison "to assure you of my readiness to do all in my power to make your accession to office easy and agreeable." The New York World commented: "President Cleveland is reported to be calm and unconcerned. This noble example which he sets will not be lost upon this country."

Days before Harrison's March 4 inauguration, a Chicago Herald editorial called for Cleveland to be the Democratic presidential nominee in 1892. "Let the good work begin," the paper said.

Cleveland said he hadn't thought about what he would do next. "My future movements are as yet wholly unsettled," he told reporters.

The former president moved to New York City and joined a prestigious law firm. In 1890, he became the second president to argue a case before the U.S. Supreme Court. He and his wife had a child, Ruth, the first of five children. "Baby Ruth" became a national celebrity.

(In 1921, a candymaker introduced a Baby Ruth candy bar, claiming it was named after Cleveland's daughter, who died of diphtheria in 1904 at age 12. It was widely believed the company was avoiding paying royalties to star baseball slugger Babe Ruth.)

While disavowing interest in running for president again, Cleveland gave about 10 speeches a year. By the time of the 1892 Democratic Convention, the party's choice for nominee was clear. "Grover's Name Towers Over All," the Pittsburgh Dispatch wrote. The election was a Cleveland-Harrison rerun.

Harrison, who was nicknamed the "Human Iceberg," was unpopular. The campaign was low-key because the first lady, Caroline Harrison, was gravely ill with tuberculosis. She died two weeks before the election.

This time Cleveland won easily. But his transition was troubled by a looming economic crisis. Harrison seemed in denial, telling Congress, "There has never been a time in our history when work was so abundant." Some historians speculate that he wanted to pin the blame on his successor. The Panic of 1893 hit just two weeks before Cleveland was inaugurated.

Nevertheless, by 1896 there was talk of a third term. Then, in June, Cleveland greeted members of the Louisville Colonels baseball team at the White House. The manager, William McGunnigle, had been a player in Buffalo when Cleveland was mayor. Cleveland made news when McGunnigle said he hoped the president would run again. Cleveland shook his head and said: "No third term for me. I couldn't stand it."

Only a few former presidents ever tried to return to the White House after being out of office. The most famous candidate was two-term President Theodore Roosevelt, who ran in 1912 for the Bull Moose Party after having a falling out with the Republican candidate, President William Howard Taft.

Roosevelt's presidential run was nearly fatal. Before a speech in Milwaukee, a New York bar owner shot Roosevelt in the chest. Fortunately, the bullet was slowed by a copy of a 50-page speech Roosevelt had stuffed inside his overcoat pocket. He delivered his 84-minute speech, telling the audience he had been shot and noting, "It takes more than that to kill a Bull Moose."

# CHAPTER SIXTEEN

# THE FIRST INVESTIGATION OF A CAPITOL ATTACK

By Ronald G. Shafer
*This column was published in the Washington Post on Oct. 20, 2021*

On Sept. 23, 1814, Rep. Richard Mentor Johnson of Kentucky, "covered with wounds and resting on crutches," rose to propose a special House committee to investigate the attack on the U.S. Capitol by the British, according to an 1849 account by a colleague, Rep. Charles J. Ingersoll of Pennsylvania.

The 33-year-old Johnson, a military hero in the ongoing War of 1812, sought an inquiry into the federal government's failure to prevent the burning of the Capitol and other Washington buildings by British troops on Aug. 24 and 25, 1814 — just as a select House committee now is probing the Jan. 6 attack on the Capitol by backers of former president Donald Trump and the inadequate protection. That committee has issued subpoenas to top Trump administration officials to testify and said it will seek to hold those who refuse to comply in criminal contempt.

If history is any guide, accountability is far from ensured.

The 1814 investigation began with promise. The House, temporarily meeting at Blodgett's Hotel in Washington, approved a special committee of three Federalists and three Democratic-Republicans, with Johnson as chairman. (Johnson would later become vice president under Martin Van Buren and attract controversy for his relationship with his common-law wife, Julia Chinn, an enslaved African American at his Kentucky plantation

The House gave the committee "the power to send for persons and papers." The panel gathered written statements from more than two dozen people, plus scores of documents.

President James Madison was exempted out of deference to his office. The highest-ranking official to testify was the secretary of state and future president, James Monroe.

Cabinet and military officials said that on July 1, 1814, Madison had ordered military preparations for a possible attack on Washington, then a modest town of about 8,000 people. Secretary of War John Armstrong Jr. insisted Baltimore would be the more likely target. Armstrong, one general told the committee, treated "with indifference if not with levity, the idea of an attack by the enemy" on the capital.

On Aug. 19, British ships moored on the Patuxent River in Southern Maryland. Intelligence reports showed British troops were heading to Washington via Bladensburg, Md., about six miles northeast of the Capitol. Gen. William Henry Winder, who headed Washington's defense, said he sent "the whole" of his troops out of the capital to meet the enemy. Most were militia volunteers from the District of Columbia and three neighboring states.

Winder said Maryland and Pennsylvania failed to provide the promised number of militia soldiers. Virginia's militia, he said, didn't reach the battlefield in time after being delayed getting arms and ammunition by a bureaucratic Army clerk who demanded signed receipts for every item. The committee report termed the mustering of forces "a great and manifest failure."

On the morning of Aug. 24, the 63-year-old Madison rode his horse to Bladensburg. Joining him were Monroe, Armstrong and Attorney General Richard Rush. William Simmons, a Bladensburg resident, later told the committee he had been scouting the area when by chance he ran into the president and the three Cabinet members as they were about to ride into the town.

Simmons said when he warned them the British were already there, Madison "exclaimed with surprise, 'The enemy in Bladensburg!' and at the same moment they all turned their horses and rode towards our troops with considerable speed." Madison moved to the back of the U.S. forces and observed the start of the Battle of Bladensburg just after noon, before riding back to Washington.

The British troops soon sent Winder's raw forces into a chaotic retreat. Winder told the committee he directed some retreating troops to rally at the Capitol, but "when I arrived at the Capitol, I found not a man had passed that way."

Winder stated that after Monroe and Armstrong rode up, the three men agreed that rather than have the "reduced and exhausted" troops defend the Capitol, it would be more strategic to send them to the heights overlooking Georgetown. The D.C. militia's general strongly disagreed. "It is impossible to do justice to the anguish evinced by the troops" on receiving the order to move on, he told the committee.

The Capitol was left undefended when British forces arrived that evening. British Adm. George Cockburn ordered his men to fire musket volleys into the Capitol, which was unoccupied because Congress wasn't in session.

Then troops rushed in and began ransacking the building. "They are in possession of the very Capitol, rioting and reveling in the sacred halls of American legislation, without fear or without danger," the United States Gazette reported.

Ingersoll wrote later that Cockburn, "in a strain of coarse levity," was rumored to have sat in the House Speaker's chair and put the question to his troops, "Shall this harbor of Yankee democracy be burned? All for it will say aye." The question "carried unanimously." The troops piled up furniture, and Cockburn set it ablaze.

FIGURE 24 BURNING OF THE CAPITOL

The British moved on to set fire to the empty president's mansion, which would later become widely known as the White House, and the Treasury building. The next morning, troops burned the War and State departments' building. After a tornado-like storm swept through Washington that day, the British headed back to their ships.

Even before the House investigation began, critics were pointing fingers. "Oh! But for a scapegoat," one newspaper said.

Armstrong resigned as secretary of war under pressure from Madison, who moved Monroe to the post. Winder was a top target. The record is clear that "the general is unfit for any important command and that to him, principally, the Enemy is indebted for his success that day," wrote the Baltimore American.

Rep. Zebulon Shipherd, a Federalist from New York, charged that "the Chief Magistrate in particular is responsible for this shameful transaction. He, his Secretary of War were on the field of battle, or rather of flight. Was it then by their orders or the order of either of them, that the metropolis was cowardly given up to be sacked by the enemy?"

Some critics accused sympathizers of the British in Washington of privately supporting the attackers. "The British faction, the Tories, the moral traitors, what are they doing?" asked the United States Gazette.

The committee completed its investigation in just over two months, delivering a 370-page report to the House on Nov. 29. To the surprise of many observers, the report avoided any conclusions or blame. Johnson "said the committee had reported all the material facts — but had left the

House and the country to decide upon the whole matter," the Hartford Courant reported.

Rep. Daniel Webster, a Federalist from New Hampshire, objected that rather than "clearing up the causes of the failure of our arms at this place," the voluminous report "was calculated (though not intended) to cover up ... what he considered to be a most disgraceful transaction," the Courant said, and "served in no degree to lead the public sentiment in respect to this disaster."

On Feb. 4, 1815, the House voted unanimously to table the report indefinitely. Then came news that Gen. Andrew Jackson had defeated the British at New Orleans, followed by mail receipt of a previously signed peace treaty, the Treaty of Ghent, ending the war.

Congress never voted on the report on the burning of the Capitol. Lawmakers shied away from "implicating so many marked personages," Ingersoll wrote in 1849. "The fall of Washington was put to rest as one of those overwhelming and incurable evils which cannot be redressed, explained or dwelt upon, but must be consigned to contemptuous amnesty or merciful oblivion."

# CHAPTER SEVENTEEN

# TEMPEST IN A TEAPOT DOME

By Ronald G. Shafer
*This column was published in the Washington Post on Jan. 15, 2022*

One inquiry was triggered by a violent invasion of the U.S. Capitol, the other by corrupt selling of federal oil leases. But both acts were assaults on democracy that led to some of the most anticipated and politically charged congressional hearings in U.S. history.

Nearly a century before a House committee's planned hearings on the Jan. 6 attack on the Capitol, a Senate panel launched hearings on a secret lease to allow private drilling in the Teapot Dome naval oil reserve field in Wyoming. The probe revealed another type of attack on democracy: the greasing of the wheels of government to benefit rich and powerful interests. The hearings uncovered brazen bribery in arguably the country's biggest political scandal until Watergate, resulting in the first imprisonment of a former Cabinet member.

What bombshells will be unearthed in the current investigation remain to be seen. The House select committee plans to hold hearings "setting out for the American people in vivid color exactly what happened, every minute of the day on January 6th, here at the Capitol and at the White House, and what led to that violent attack," Republican Rep. Liz Cheney (Wyo.), the panel's vice chairwoman, has promised.

"I think this is one of the single most important congressional investigations in history," Cheney said.

That label certainly applies to the Teapot Dome probe. The saga began on April 14, 1922, when the Wall Street Journal reported that officials in the administration of Republican President Warren G. Harding had secretly leased drilling rights at Teapot Dome, named for a nearby teapot-shaped rock, to the oil magnate Harry Sinclair.

FIGURE 25 ALBERT FALL

Teapot Rock, a distinctive sedimentary rock formation in Natrona County, Wyo., that lent its name to a nearby oil field that became notorious as the focus of the Teapot Dome brouhaha in the early 20th century.

The lease was issued without competitive bidding by Interior Secretary Albert Bacon Fall, a former U.S. senator from New Mexico. It was later revealed that Fall also had leased two California naval oil reserve fields to the oil baron Edward Doheny. Combined, the three leases were valued at about $200 million, equal to more than $3 billion now.

The Senate immediately voted to investigate the Teapot Dome lease. The probe focused on the 60-year-old Fall, who "mildly resembles a Western bandit with his black hat and his sunburnt face" and "smokes the worst cigars in Washington," the Brooklyn Eagle reported.

The Senate investigation got bogged down as Fall inundated the committee with more than 5,000 documents — similar to the 6,000 emails and documents provided to the Jan. 6 panel by former White House chief of staff Mark Meadows, before he stopped cooperating. In early 1923, Fall resigned to return to private business at his ranch in Three Rivers, N.M.

Republicans, who controlled the Senate, were wary about pressing too hard against one of their own, and they didn't mind giving the hearings the appearance of partisanship, so they let Democratic Sen. Thomas Walsh (Mont.) take the lead. Senate GOP leaders — like House Republican leaders now — then tried to derail the investigation. Harding's attorney general, Harry Daugherty, even sent federal agents to Montana to try to dig up dirt on Walsh, who suspected his phone was tapped.

Harding supported Fall and said he had approved the oil lease. The story faded by the summer of 1923, when the president and his wife left on a trip to the Alaska Territory. On Aug. 2, Harding suffered a fatal stroke at the San Francisco Palace Hotel. Vice President Calvin Coolidge became president.

FIGURE 26 SENATOR THOMAS WALSH

Senate hearings finally began on Oct. 23, 1923, in the same Senate caucus room where the Watergate hearings would take place 50 years later. (The journalist Richard Strout, who covered both Teapot Dome and Watergate, wasn't far off the mark when he coined "Strout's Law" stipulating that "every 50 years we have a great scandal, and watch out for 2023.")

Fall testified that the Wyoming lease was perfectly legal and good for the nation. With no new revelations, a popular syndicated newspaper column raised the inevitable question: "And is that Teapot Dome oil row a tempest in a teapot?"

Walsh, a former prosecutor, kept digging. In December, he discovered startling information about mysterious payments to Fall. "The hearings suddenly were the hottest ticket in Washington," Laton McCartney wrote in his book "The Teapot Dome Scandal."

On Jan. 21, 1924, "the thrill of the hearing exceeded anything the Capitol has staged in years," the Baltimore Sun reported. The surprise star witness was Archibald Roosevelt, a son of the late President Theodore Roosevelt and the younger brother of Assistant Navy Secretary Theodore Roosevelt Jr.

"Archie" Roosevelt testified that he had just resigned as a vice president of Harry Sinclair's oil company after Sinclair's confidential secretary told him about "a $68,000 check paid to the foreman of Secretary Fall's ranch." That is equal to $1.1 million now. The secretary then testified as well, denying Roosevelt's claim and saying that he had told Roosevelt that Fall had merely been given "six or eight cows." Walsh immediately called Roosevelt back up to testify again, and Roosevelt said he was "dead sure" what he had heard. (The secretary later conceded that Roosevelt was right.)

Three days later, the committee heard from Doheny, the owner of the California oil leases. Doheny admitted to making an interest-free "loan" (it was widely interpreted as a bribe) of $100,000 — or $1.7 million now — to Fall for improvements on his ranch. The multimillionaire said that $100,000 "was a bagatelle to me" and that the loan was simply "a personal transaction based on old-time friendship." He said his son Edward "Ned" Doheny Jr. and Ned's assistant delivered the money in cash in a black satchel to Fall in Washington in late 1921.

"The Teapot Dome scandal which for a long time was 'just' another Senate investigation… has become almost overnight a throbbing drama of politics, high finance and intrigue," United Press International reported. Coolidge, who had been silent on the controversy, appointed two special prosecutors, a Republican and a Democrat.

In March, Sinclair was called back to testify, but this time, like Meadows and other figures in the current inquiry, he refused to answer questions and was charged with contempt of Congress.

Coolidge managed to distance himself from the scandal, and that November, he was elected on the slogan "Keep Cool With Coolidge."

Walsh led one final round of highly publicized hearings in early 1928. Fall's son- in-law testified that he had delivered $233,000 in World War I Liberty Bonds and $36,000 in cash from Sinclair to Fall after the Teapot Dome lease was concluded. The $269,000 total would be $4.5 million today.

The Teapot Dome inquiries had lasting impact. In 1927, the Supreme Court voided the private leases. The court also for the first time upheld Congress's right to compel witnesses to testify, in a case where former Attorney General Daugherty's brother declined to appear before a committee probing Daugherty's failure to prosecute Teapot Dome cases. In 1929, the court also upheld Sinclair's conviction that year for contempt of Congress; he was sentenced to 10 months in prison for contempt and for jury tampering in a related trial.

Fall, bankrupt and reliant on a wheelchair, was convicted of taking bribes and sentenced to one year in prison. But Sinclair and Edward Doheny were acquitted of bribery. In early 1929, Ned Doheny and his assistant, who were to testify at Fall's trial, were found shot to death at Greystone Mansion, Ned's Beverly Hills estate. Police ruled it a murder-suicide by the assistant.

The scandal became part of Harding's legacy. In their book "The Teapot Dome Scandal," M.R. Werner and John Starr wrote that when a committee picked a design for Harding's tomb in Marion, Ohio, one member exclaimed, "My God, gentlemen, you aren't going to take this?" Asked why not, the man responded: "Stick a handle on here, and what have you got? A teapot."

# CHAPTER EIGHTEEN

# WITH MALICE TOWARD NONE

By Ronald G. Shafer
*This column was published in the Washington Post on Jan.20, 2021*

In delivering an inauguration speech to try to heal a bitterly divided nation, President Joe Biden faced perhaps the greatest challenge since Abraham Lincoln in 1865.

In his "America United" address, Biden spoke "about the need to bring the country together during an unprecedented moment of crisis." His address followed an attack on the U.S. Capitol by supporters of a president who still won't accept defeat and refused to attend his successor's swearing-in and a pandemic that has killed hundreds of thousands of Americans.

In his second inauguration on March 4, 1865, Lincoln sought to begin the healing of a divided country emerging from a bloody Civil War that took more than 700,000 lives in the North and the South.

The new dome of the Capitol with the Statue of Freedom on top gleamed in the bright sunlight behind the 56-year-old Lincoln as he stepped forward to deliver his address. The clearing sky seemed symbolic of the ending of the dark war to the special correspondent for the New York Times, poet Walt Whitman.

"As the president came out on the capitol portico, a curious little white cloud, the only in that part of the sky, appeared like a hovering bird, right over him," Whitman wrote.

The crowd of 40,000 people roared as Lincoln moved to the front of the high platform wearing a plain black frock coat. Spectators stood in mud following a rainstorm that had swept through the city shortly before the ceremony.

FIGURE 27 LINCOLN'S 1865 INAUGURATION

Lincoln began by noting the contrast to his first inauguration in 1861 when platoons of troops guarded the ceremony as war approached. The scene, with sharp shooters stationed atop houses, was much like the backdrop of the 25,000 National Guard members protecting the inauguration of Biden and Vice President Kamala Harris.

"While the inaugural address was being delivered from this place, devoted altogether to saving the Union without war, insurgent agents were in the city seeking to destroy it without war — seeking to dissolve the Union," Lincoln said. "Both parties deprecated war, but one of them would make war rather than let the nation survive, and the other would accept war rather than let it perish, and the war came."

Lincoln moved to the issue that had split the union.One-eighth of the population were enslaved people, localized in the South. "These slaves constituted a peculiar and powerful interest," he said. "All knew that this interest was somehow the cause of the war."

But the Great Emancipator didn't let the North off the hook. "To strengthen, perpetuate, and extend this interest was the object for which the insurgents would rend the Union even by war," he said, "while the government claimed no right to do more than to restrict the territorial enlargement of it."

FIGURE 28 ABRAHAM LINCOLN

Lincoln invoked biblical references both to condemn slavery and to seek healing. "It may seem strange that any men should dare to ask a just God's assistance in wringing their bread from the sweat of other men's faces," he said, "but let us judge not, that we be not judged."

The large number of African Americans in the crowd "seemed to have been the only portion of the assembly which was much moved by the Scriptural speech of the ex-rail splitter," one newspaper said. They responded with "Bless the Lord" in "a low murmur at the end of almost every sentence."

The inauguration was the first since Lincoln had issued the Emancipation Proclamation freeing enslaved people on Jan. 1, 1863. Congress had just passed the 13th Amendment to the Constitution abolishing slavery. For the first time, African American soldiers marched in an inauguration parade.

Pride was evident in the faces of Black citizens, newspapers wrote. "You ought to have been on the steps of the Capitol on Inauguration day, and seen the faces of the listening crowd," one Black man wrote later in the African American newspaper the Liberator. "If I were to live to the age of Methuselah, I could not expect ever to witness such a spectacle again."

Though the Union was near final victory over the Confederacy, Lincoln didn't gloat. The prayers of neither side have been "answered fully," he said. "Fondly do we hope, fervently do we pray, that this mighty scourge of war may speedily pass away."

Lincoln's speech lasted only about six minutes. At just over 700 words it was second only to President George Washington's remarks of 135 words in 1793 as the shortest inauguration address.

As the crowd broke up and mingled, it was clear that it would take more than a speech to heal divisions.

"It seemed as if there was a reaction from the anti-slavery sentiments of the inaugural, and every Negro boy got an extra push on account of his color," the New York Tribune reported. "Soldiers knocked Negro women roughly about and called them very uncomplimentary names."

Lincoln returned to the White House about 3 p.m. "He was in his plain two-horse barouche, and looked very much worn and tired," Whitman wrote in the Times.

"The lines, indeed, of vast responsibilities, intricate questions, and demands of life and death, cut deeper than ever upon his dark brown face; yet all the old goodness, tenderness, sadness, and canny shrewdness underneath the furrows."

Lincoln was unsure how his speech would be received. Black abolition leader Frederick Douglass was invited to that night's White House reception, and the president waved him over.

FIGURE 29 FREDERICK DOUGLASS

"Here comes my friend Douglass," Lincoln said. "I saw you in the crowd today, listening to my inaugural address; how did you like it?"

"Mr. Lincoln," Douglass responded after a hesitation, "that was a sacred effort."

Douglass later said that he had "a vague presentiment" as he watched Lincoln's inauguration. "I felt that there was murder in the air."

Another man in the crowd that day was a popular actor and Confederate sympathizer named John Wilkes Booth. Historians speculate that Booth had considered shooting Lincoln at the inauguration.

On April 9, Confederate Gen. Robert E. Lee surrendered to Union Gen. Ulysses S. Grant at Appomattox Court House in Virginia. The war was finally over. To celebrate, Lincoln and his wife, Mary, decided to attend a play, "Our American Cousin," at Ford's Theatre in Washington on the night of April 14.

The rest is history. Booth slipped up the stairs to Lincoln's balcony box overlooking the stage and shot the president in the back of the head. Lincoln died the next morning.

Lincoln's inauguration speech lives on, however, as an eloquent call for mutual forgiveness. A closing line "should be engraved on every heart," one newspaper of the day said:

"With malice toward none, with charity for all, with firmness in the right as God gives us to see the right, let us strive on to finish the work we are in, to bind up the nation's wounds."

# CHAPTER NINETEEN

## AMERICA'S FIRST COLUMBUS DAY

By Ronald G. Shafer
*This column was published in the Washington Post on Oct. 10, 2021*

The first national Columbus Day was proclaimed in 1892 by Republican President Benjamin Harrison to celebrate the 400th anniversary of Italian-born explorer Christopher Columbus's supposed discovery of America.

But for Harrison, it served another purpose: to help resolve a diplomatic crisis with Italy — and gain support among Italian American voters — after rioters in New Orleans lynched 11 Italian immigrants the year before.

Columbus Day has come under fire in recent years by critics alleging that Columbus was responsible for the enslavement and massacre of Indigenous people. Some cities, including Columbus, Ohio, have pulled down statues of the explorer. And President Biden made history Friday by announcing he would commemorate Indigenous Peoples' Day alongside the Columbus holiday.

A group of Italian American organizations is countering the attacks on Columbus Day with advertisements denying the claims against Columbus and urging a broader observance of the holiday by "celebrating all Americans."

The first national Columbus Day grew out of a backdrop of violence. In March 1891, a jury in New Orleans acquitted six Italian immigrants charged with the murder of the local police chief. Rumors spread that jurors had been bribed by powerful Italian families coming to be known as the Mafia.

The next morning, thousands of people — many of them leading citizens of the Crescent City — descended on Orleans Parish Prison, where the six Italian defendants and 13 other Italian suspects were being held.

"'Bring 'em out, we'll kill 'em,' came the cry from a thousand throats," the New Orleans Times-Democrat reported. A group of armed men broke into the prison and shot nine of the defendants dead, one falling with 42 bullets in his body, the paper said. The mob took two others to the city square, when one man was hanged on a lamp post and another on a tree.

The article ran under the headline "Avenged." At a time of widespread discrimination against Italian immigrants, many news reports followed the theme that the killings were justified. The Associated Press said of the killers: "It was not an unruly midnight mob. It was simply a sullen determined body of citizens who took into their own hands what justice had ignominiously failed to do."

The New York Times wrote that "while every good citizen" would agree that "this affair is to be deplored, it would be difficult to find any individual who would confess that privately he deplores it very much." U.S. Civil Service Commissioner Theodore Roosevelt, in a letter to his sister, said of the revengeful violence, "Personally, I think it a rather good thing."

But Italian Americans and leaders of the kingdom of Italy were outraged. Italy broke off diplomatic relations and recalled its ambassador from Washington. The Harrison administration in turn removed the U.S. legation from Rome. There was even talk of war.

Harrison remained silent on the matter until his December message to Congress, when he called the murders "a most deplorable and discreditable incident" and an "offense against law and humanity." The next April, he agreed to Italy's demands to pay an indemnity to survivors of three victims who were citizens of Italy.

Secretary of State James Blaine, in a telegram to Italian officials about "the lamentable massacre at New Orleans," said that at the president's instruction, the U.S. government would pay a total indemnity of $25,000 — equal to about $760,000 today.

Italy accepted the offer, but Harrison's action drew criticism.

"Peace at Any Price. Uncle Sam Humbles Itself Before Italy," declared a headline in the Los Angeles Herald. Some lawmakers argued that Harrison exceeded his executive power by acting without Congress's approval.

With a looming election rematch against former president Grover Cleveland, whom Harrison had defeated in 1888, politics was naturally on the president's mind.

FIGURE 30 BENJAMIN HARRISON

One factor in Harrison's action was "the approaching Presidential election and the necessity the President feels under of repairing his political fences in every direction," the Brooklyn Citizen wrote. "He does not want to have the Italian vote massed against him."

Diplomatic relations with Italy resumed, but the Italians were still upset that the United States didn't prosecute the murderers.

The calendar provided an opportunity to further placate the Italians. Many communities already were planning to celebrate the 400th anniversary of Columbus's arrival in the New World.

A New York minister, Francis Bellamy, met with Harrison to urge a national holiday to promote patriotism among American schoolchildren. Bellamy, a self-described Christian socialist, had written "The Pledge of Allegiance" for the occasion.

With Harrison's support, Congress passed a resolution calling for a one-time holiday for Americans to celebrate Columbus on Oct. 21 "by public demonstration and by suitable exercises in their schools and other places of assembly." Harrison issued his proclamation on July 21, urging efforts to "impress upon our youth the patriotic duties of American citizenship."

Celebrations took place across the country. The biggest was in New York City on Oct. 12, the date that Columbus had first made landfall in the Western Hemisphere when he arrived in the Bahamas. More than 1 million spectators cheered a parade featuring 40,000 marching military men in uniform, the New York World reported. The New York Times called the turnout "the greatest crowd New York ever held."

An army of 1,000 Native Americans brought up the rear of the parade, the New York Times said. They were on foot and wore the "every-day stage style of Indian costume with red blankets, painted faces and feathered head gear."The next day, a crowd gathered for the unveiling of a 14-foot statue of Columbus atop a 27.5-foot granite column. The statue at Columbus Circle still stands.

Harrison wasn't able to take political advantage of the celebrations. He declined an invitation to attend the New York City festivities because his wife, Caroline, was dying of tuberculosis. The following week, he bowed out of the groundbreaking for the 1893 Columbian World's Fair in Chicago.

Cleveland also canceled his visit to the World's Fair out of deference to Harrison. But the former president had a front-row seat on the reviewing stand at the New York City parade. The next month, Cleveland defeated Harrison to become the only president ever to be elected to two nonconsecutive terms.

Columbus Day became a permanent national holiday in 1934 when Congress, after lobbying by the Knights of Columbus, authorized President Franklin D. Roosevelt to declare Oct. 12 as the designated date. In 1971, Columbus Day was made a federal holiday on the second Monday in October.

That year, celebrations again took place across America, but in San Francisco, 30 Native Americans protested. Their leader, wearing a Chippewa tribe ceremonial headdress, called Columbus Day a day of mourning for Indians until "we are given the same opportunity to achieve the same social, economic and educational levels as the rest of those who call themselves Americans."

FIGURE 31 NEW YORK COLUMBUS DAY PARADE

# CHAPTER TWENTY

# HAPPY FRANKSGIVING

By Ronald G. Shafer
*This column was published in the Washington Post on Nov. 24, 2021*

In 1939, half of America celebrated Thanksgiving, and the other half celebrated "Franksgiving."

To boost the economy, President Franklin D. Roosevelt moved Thanksgiving up a week to create an extra seven days of Christmas shopping. Talk about a New Deal.

Turkey Day traditionalists cried foul. "We heartily disapprove," said the chairman of the annual celebration commemorating the 1621 harvest feast by the Pilgrims and Native Americans in Plymouth,Mass., that became Thanksgiving. "We here in Plymouth consider the day sacred." (Members of the Wampanoag Nation tend to see it differently.)

Critics dubbed Roosevelt's holiday "Franksgiving." The issue divided Americans along political lines. Alf Landon, the Republican whom Roosevelt had trounced in the 1936 election, accused FDR of arbitrarily acting "with the omnipotence of a Hitler."

But the business world was delighted with the change. The earlier date will "spread the 'shop-early' movement and be beneficial to customer, clerk and retailer," said the president of the Merchants and Manufacturers Association. The president of Lord & Taylor predicted that the change could generate as much as $1 billion of additional business, the equivalent of nearly $20 billion today.

Thanksgiving had mostly been observed on the last Thursday of November since President Abraham Lincoln proclaimed it a national holiday in 1863. In 1939, November had five Thursdays, and the last one, on Nov. 30, left a short time for the Christmas shopping season. (Back then, retailers did not dare start promoting the Christmas season until after Thanksgiving.)

In August 1939, Roosevelt announced he was moving Thanksgiving to Nov. 23 at the urging of retailers. The president said the idea sounded "silly" but decided to defer to the merchants, the Associated Press reported.

The late announcement played havoc with planned Thanksgiving events such as rivalry football games, parades, church services and school closings. "College catalogs are already in print. Class schedules are arranged," the president of the American Association of Collegiate Registrars telegraphed to Roosevelt. Students will end up skipping classes both holiday weekends, he complained.

Even some turkey sellers protested the short notice. "Your contemplated change will be injurious to many producers and disrupt marketing plans of processors and distributors," wired the president of the National Poultry, Butter and Egg Association.

Comedians had something new to chew on. On Jack Benny's popular radio show, Benny's wife, Mary Livingstone, read a poem: "Thanksgiving, you're a little mixed up, aren't you, kid?"

FIGURE 32 FRANKLIN & ELEANOR ROOSEVELT

Public opinion split along political lines. A Gallup Poll showed Democrats favored the switch 52 percent to 48 percent, while Republicans opposed it 79 percent to 21 percent. Overall, Americans opposed the change 62 to 38.

Many GOP governors vowed to keep the traditional Thanksgiving date. The result was two Thanksgivings: 23 states and the District of Columbia went with Nov. 23, while 22 states stuck with Nov. 30. Three states — Colorado, Mississippi and Texas — observed both dates.

Thousands of protest letters poured in to the White House. But Roosevelt stuck to his drumsticks.

On Nov. 23, he dined on Thanksgiving turkey in Warm Springs, Ga. The president's remarks at the dinner reflected the day's grim headlines about 30 British sailors being killed when their battleship hit a German mine in the Thames during the widening European war with Nazi Germany. "Well, we have a war," Roosevelt said. "I hope by next spring we won't have one."

Thanksgiving celebrations took place across the country. In New York City, more than 1 million people turned out for the Macy's Thanksgiving Day Parade, led by a 50-foot Santa Claus. Philadelphia's Toyland Parade drew 500,000 people to see 25 bands, 1,000 clowns and African American movie star and dancer Bill Robinson, "who danced his way along the parade route as the special guest of honor," the Philadelphia Inquirer reported.

In Hollywood, gossip columnist Louella Parsons reported that actor "Ronnie" Reagan was thankful for landing the starring role in the new movie "For the Rich They Sing," which she described as "a comedy with a political slant."

Three of the four Republican governors at the New England Conference at Boston's Statler Hotel dined on turkey. When Gov. Lewis Barrows of Maine was handed a carving knife, he responded, "No, thanks. I've brought a can of sardines with me."

Long before Black Friday, merchants ran Christmas ads on the Friday after the early Thanksgiving. In The Washington Post, the Woodward & Lothrop department store promoted "Christmas Cherishables," such as a "Christmasy Evening in Paris" perfume. In New York, Macy's pictured Santa Claus in an ad for family games, such as a "talking table" called the Voodoo.

FDR's early Turkey Day goosed early Christmas buying. "Yule Sales Off to Flying Start in First Week," declared a Post headline.

On Nov. 30, the rest of the country observed a relatively low-key Thanksgiving. Plymouth staged its traditional Thanksgiving ceremony, which officials pointedly noted was designed to "save the day from exploitation and desecration."

The double Thanksgiving continued in 1940, after Roosevelt won an unprecedented third term. This time, 32 states joined in the early observance. Political division continued: A Warner Bros. "Merrie Melodies" cartoon movie showed a Thanksgiving calendar marked Nov. 21 for Democrats and Nov. 28 for Republicans.

In late 1941, after the United States had entered World War II, Congress approved and Roosevelt signed a proclamation to set Thanksgiving, starting in 1942, as the fourth Thursday in November, where it remains today. Roosevelt said at a news conference that he was swayed by government economic reports showing the early Thanksgivings didn't boost total Christmas sales much after all.

"Waving a handful of statistics, graphs, reports and comments," the International News Service reported, "the President admitted that moving up the date of Thanksgiving a week had been a complete turkey."

FIGURE 33 THANKSGIVINGS 1940

# CHAPTER TWENTY-ONE

# SANTA WORE BLUE

By Ronald G. Shafer
*This column was published in the Washington*
*Post on December 23, 2021*

The modern image of Santa Claus first appeared during the Civil War. Santa sided with the North.

He made his debut on the cover of Harper's Weekly for Christmas 1862. A drawing shows a white-bearded Santa Claus, wearing a fur coat with stars and stripes. But he's not filling stockings for the kids. Instead, he's handing out presents at a Union army camp — and dangling a puppet with a rope around its neck. The puppet resembles Confederate President Jefferson Davis.

The drawing was by 22-year-old Thomas Nast, who was born in Germany and came to New York with his family at age 6. Nast said he based his Santa on a German version of Saint Nicholas, Pelze-Nicol. The artist later became famous for his cartoons lampooning William "Boss" Tweed of New York City's corrupt Tammany Hall political machine.

But he initially gained attention for his drawings championing the Union cause, including the one that introduced his Santa. President Abraham Lincoln called Nast the Union's "best recruiting sergeant," adding, "His emblematic cartoons have never failed to arouse enthusiasm and patriotism and have always seemed to come just when these articles were getting scarce."

FIGURE 34 NAST'S UNION CAMP

The Harper's 1862 Christmas edition included another Nast drawing, "Christmas Eve," showing Santa Claus and his sleigh on the roof of a house where stockings hang from a mantel and a woman is kneeling in prayer beside a bed with two sleeping children. Another panel shows her husband in a Union uniform sitting next to a tree, holding a rifle and gazing at family photos.

Nast's elaborate illustrations were pro-Union and anti-slavery. After Lincoln issued the Emancipation Proclamation in January 1863, a Nast drawing titled "Emancipation" envisioned a brighter future for Black Americans. It shows images of enslaved people being beaten and branded, but the center picture portrays a happy Black family gathered around a fireplace with a picture of Lincoln on the mantel.

FIGURE 35 NAST'S EMANCIPADTION

Nast's drawings, one newspaper of the day noted, "tell more in their silent way and point to a stronger moral than could a hundred stump orators." But they also drew "scores of threatening letters to the Harper office from the infuriated South, and Nast would have been burned at the stake had he been captured during the occasional trips he made to the front," Albert Bigelow Paine wrote in his 1904 book, "Th. Nast: His Period And His Pictures."

In 1864, Nast backed the reelection of Lincoln, a Republican. After the Democratic convention adopted a platform that seemed to call for peace at any price, Nast responded with a drawing called "Compromise with the South." It shows a kneeling Lady Columbia — a precursor to Uncle Sam — weeping as a one-legged Union soldier on a crutch reluctantly shakes hands with a triumphant Confederate officer over a grave marker that reads, "In Memory Of Our Union Heroes Who Fell In A Useless War."

Lincoln supporters distributed copies to voters. "The good the cartoon accomplished was held to be incalculable," the New York Times wrote.

Nast attended Lincoln's second inauguration in March 1865. A month later, he published a drawing showing Lady Columbia grieving over the coffin of the assassinated president. The illustration was published in nearly every newspaper in the United States.

The cartoonist assailed President Andrew Johnson's undoing of Lincoln's Reconstruction. One multi-paneled illustration shows Johnson as a snake charmer playing a flute as two copperhead snakes coil death grips around a Black man writhing on the floor.

Nast became known as the "Father of Political Cartoonists." He created the elephant as the symbol for the Republican Party and popularized the Democratic Party symbol of a donkey that started with President Andrew Jackson.

In 1868, Nast supported the presidential nomination of Gen. Ulysses S. Grant. The artist drew a cartoon showing two pedestals in front of the White House entrance. Grant is pictured behind the Republican pedestal, and the Democratic pedestal still awaits a nominee. The caption reads: "Match Him." When Grant won, he credited the sword of Union Gen. Philip Sheridan "and the pencil of Thomas Nast."

In 1876, Nast backed Republican Rutherford B. Hayes against Democrat Samuel J. Tilden. The deadlocked election result was disputed after the suppression of Black Republican voters in Southern states. White Southerners threatened violence if the election was "stolen" from Tilden.

"Hotheads shouted, 'On to Washington' and 'Minute Men' began to prepare to march," John Chalmers Vinson wrote in his book "Thomas Nast, Political Cartoonist". Amid "threats of insurrection," Vinson wrote, Congress appointed a 15-member Electoral Commission to determine the winner.

A Nast drawing represented the Democrats as a pair of disembodied hands, one holding a gun and the other wielding a bull whip, above a poster reading "Tilden Elected Or Blood." When the panel gave Hayes the victory by one electoral vote in early 1877, Nast drew a Republican elephant in bandages and on a crutch with the caption, " 'Another such victory, and I am undone' - Pyrrhus."

Nast turned against Hayes when he agreed in the Compromise of 1877 to withdraw federal troops from the South, ushering in Jim Crow segregation and disenfranchisement. An 1879 Nast cartoon attacking literacy tests in the South shows an African American man sitting next to a shed where a semiliterate White man is writing on a bulletin board, "The blak man orter be eddikated afore he kin vote with us wites." The message is signed "Mr. Solid South."

The cartoonist had his critics. Nast's "brutal, meat-ax style" represents "all that is course and rough and low, without a trace of the good in humanity or a ray of light," the Nashville Daily American editorialized in 1876. "His cartoons have not proved a happy adjunct to politics."

Meanwhile, Nast expanded his image of Santa Claus in annual Christmas issues of Harper's Weekly.

FIGURE 38 NAST'S SANTA

The jolly old man grew chubbier, his beard grew longer, and he began wearing a fur-lined hat. Nast's Santa also kept up with the times. After the widespread introduction of telephones in the early 1880s, a Nast cartoon shows Santa .talking to a child on a phone from his workshop at the North Pole. "Hello, Little One," he says

Nast and Harper's parted ways in 1885. By the 1890s, the cartoonist's popularity had waned. A financial setback nearly bankrupted him.

In May 1902, President Theodore Roosevelt, a Nast fan, appointed the artist consul general at Guayaquil, Ecuador. Nast caught yellow fever there and died in December at age 62.

After his death, a brief controversy arose over whether Nast had created the modern image of Santa Claus or the image had been around since the early 1800s. But history has overwhelmingly credited Nast. In a letter to the New York Times, biographer Paine wrote: "Mr. Nast himself never doubted having been the first to present in picture the merry, fat, fur-clad, pipe-smoking Pelze-nicol of his childhood."

# ABOUT THE AUTHOR

Ron Shafer is a native of Columbus, Ohio, where he grew up with his parents Mary and Glenn Shafer and his siblings Jeanette, Mike, Sharron, Linda and Danny. He was a member of the first graduating class at the new Eastmoor High School, where the football field is named after alum and two-time Heisman Trophy winner Archie Griffith.

He is a graduate of Ohio State University's class of 1962 that also included golfer Jack Nicklaus and basketball players Jerry Lucas, John Havlicek and Bobby Knight. He was Editor-in-Chief of the campus newspaper, the Lantern. Colleagues included Len Downie, later the Executive Editor of the Washington Post, and folk singer Phil Ochs.

Ron was the first Ohio State Journalism School student ever hired by the Wall Street Journal, where he worked for 38 years in Chicago, Detroit and Washington, D.C. He became the Journal's Washington political features editor and writer of the page one column The Washington Wire.

In Detroit, Ron married Barbara Lucas in 1968, and they adopted Kathryn and Ryan. Barb died of breast cancer in 1993, six years after Ryan was killed at age 16 in a drug-related traffic accident. Ron wrote about Ryan in the Wall Street Journal and in People Magazine.

In 1998, he married entrepreneur Mary Rogers. He is stepfather to their children Dan and Kaitlin. Ron and Mary now live in Williamsburg, Va. They have six grandchildren: Katie's Kaylie; Kaitlin and John Black's Veronica and Skylar; Emma Black; and Dan and Kate's Teddy and Caroline.

# OTHER BOOKS BY RON SHAFER

How To Get Your Car Repaired Without Getting Gypped with Margaret Bresnahan Carlson, Simon & Shuster

The Complete Book of Home Buying with Michael Sumichrast, Dow Jones Books

The New Complete Book of Home Buying with Michael Sumichrast, McGraw-Hill

Where Will You Live Tomorrow? with Michael Sumichrast, Dow Jones Books

The History of the McLean Little League

Letters To Home. Mary Shafer The Memoirs of Mary Kaelber Shafer

The Carnival Campaign. How The Rollicking 1840 Campaign Of Tippecanoe and Tyler Too Changed Presidential Elections Forever, Chicago Review Press

When The Dodgers Were Bridegrooms. Gunner McGunnigle And the Back To Back Pennants of the 1889 and 1890 Brooklyn Bridegrooms. McFarland Publishing

Minor Memos. The WackySide of Politics and Power from the Wall Street Journal's Washington Wire. Andrews and McMeel.

Made in the USA
Middletown, DE
15 September 2022

10543399R00070